LEARNING AIRPORT STRATEGIES

JOHN LOK

Contents

Preface

Introduction
Any countries aiports ought need to implement in order to achieve excellent service to satisfy travel passengers their changing air planes or waiting air plans to fly to other countries need in whose short time airport staying time. However, one excellent service airport can let travelers to feel the country's airport can provide comfortable staying service , transfer another air plane from gate, shopping or eating entertainment satisfactory feeling. So, one effective airport strategy ought need to plan in order to implement satisfactory airport service performance to raise global travellers choose to go to the country to travel or stay to transfer another air plane. In my this book , I shall attempt to explain some useful airport strategy plan to let readers to understand.

Prologue

CHAPTER ONE

Implementing airport facility management strategy

Why airport needs to implement FM strategy?
Any organizations ought need to implement FM strategy. Even, any airport which is one providing air planes to fly and stay organization, it also need to provide FM service facility in order to satisfy global traveller passenger individual need when he/she is waiting in the country's airport before he/she catch air plane to fly to another country.
Firstly, we need to know that what organizational FM service means ?
Facility management can help any organizations to reduce
maintenance service expenditure, include airport air plan providing staying and flying organizations?

Facility management provides a variety of non core operations and maintenance services to support any organizations' operation. For logistic organization example, it is possible to provide effective maintenance service to warehouse in order to reduce warehouse facilities to be damaged to bring to spend to buy any new equipment facilities expenditure. So, when the logistic company's warehouse facilities can be maintenance to be the best quality. Then, they can be used these warehouses' machines facilities again. Their performance can assist workers to manufacture any products to keep the most efficiently an raising the best production performance in whole manufacturing process. Then, this logistic company's facility management department can bring to avoid purchase any new machine facilities expenditure spending. One to these warehouses' production machine facilities are kept in the best production performance environment even in long term production need.
The logistic industry's facility management department can create cost savings and efficiency of the warehouse's workplaces. It's machines

facilities (production machines) are dealt with the maintenance management of the physical assets maintenance service. FM (facilities management) has been being applied to industrial facilities in logistic and warehouse industry long term as well as maintenance plays a significant role to ensure the full service and the warehousing system, including both building components and equipment in warehouse.

Maintenance service is needed to bring a certain level of availability and reliability of a warehouse facilities system and its components and its ability perform to a standard level of quality. So , it seems that logistic industry's warehouse asset cost reducing. It depends on whether it has one facility management department to provide maintenance service to itself warehouse workplace's production machine facilities and warehouse building itself in order to let workers t feel the manufacturing machines can bring good manufacturing performance to assist them to produce any products in one safe warehouse workplace environment. Hence, the performance measurement of warehouse maintenance issue will be valued to be consider to every warehouse manager and facility manager in logistic industry.

In logistic industry, (FM) works at two level on the one hand, it provides a safe and efficient working environment, which is essential to influence warehouse workers whether how they perform to do their manufacturing tasks or logistic goods delivery tasks in warehouse. When they feel the warehouse is safe environment to work. They will not need to consider anywhere has risk to cause they die by accident in warehouse. Hence, they can concentrate on doing their every tasks . On the other hand, it can involve strategic issues, such as property (warehouse workplace and management, strategy property decision and warehouse facility, e.g. manufacturing machine, facility maintenance and checking planning and maintenance planning development.

However, reducing the operating expense issue will be the main aim when the logistic company feels that it has need to set up one in-house facility management department to carry on any maintenance service for its warehouses' any workplace property and manufacturing machines facilities. So, when the logistic company decides to implement one facility management department, it needs to ensure its facility management department can bring the minimum level of keeping manufacturing performance and efficiency to its warehouses' any manufacturing machines and warehouses' property to avoid to be damaged in short term, such as loss of business due to failure in service, provision of project to customer satisfaction, provision of safe environment, effective utilisation of workplace space, e.g. warehouse effectiveness and communication between the workers and the logistic managers in the warehouse workplace , due to the warehouse's space is not enough maintenance service reliability to the logistic company's warehouse, responsiveness of the warehouse's worker individual negative emotion problem, due to he/she often feels need to work in one unsafe warehouse working environment. Hence, it seems that poor or unsafe warehouse working environment can influence workers feel negative emotion to work to bring low efficiency (inefficiency) or under productive performance in warehouse. It has relationship to influence they to bring psychological negative emotion feeling to work when the organization lacks one effective warehouse management repairing service to be provided to the warehouse's facilities and properties' maintenance needs in order to avoid ineffective measurement and misleading of performance.

Hence, the logistic company's facilities management department often needs to be reviewed whether its maintenance service level is passed to achieve the lowest repair (maintenance) service standard to its warehouse itself property and manufacturing machine or warehouse delivery tool facilities or warehouse lamps' light whether is enough to let workers to see anything clearly to avoid accident occurrence or see anything to work clearly or the warehouse space areas are enough to let they can have enough space to walk or communicate to their team supervisors or deliver any goods more easily in the short distance between the worker's sending goods location and the delivering goods destination in order to avoid because the lacking enough space to cause the accident occurrence , due to the space is not enough to let they deliver their goods to any locations in warehouse.

Hence, it seems logistic company's (FM) department can contribute to the organization's mission, such as avoiding warehouse accident occurrence, inefficiency, not enough and unavailability of the facility for future needs when the warehouse lacks enough space areas to bring poor performance of facility and dangerous warehouse itself property in warehouse, e.g. safe and reliable operations of material handling equipment and maintenance of warehouse facilities, grounds, security system, utilities, plumbing, heating , enough lighting system, air conditioning, warming heater, fire protection, security system alarm etc. facilities in warehouse.

Hence, it seems that if the logistic company expected to reduce to spend lot of excessive manufacturing machine purchase expenditure, lose of workers' life or bring workplace accidents , due to poor warehouse workplace environment, even bringing lawsuit compensation claim loss , due to the worker individual accident or death is caused from the poor warehouse facilities, or bring negative emotion to let the workers feel they are working in unsafe warehouse workplace environment. Then, it ought choose to set up on facility management department in order to provide enough maintenance service to its warehouse to avoid these non essential expenditure causing , due to these poor warehouse facilities factors.

Hence any logistic company ought choose to set up one itself in -house facility management department, it be better than outsourcing its all facilities service to one facility management (maintenance service provider) to help it to deal any kinds of maintenance service in warehouse. Because it is long term maintenance need to its warehouse's any machines and warehouse itself properties. If it chose to find one outsourcing facilitiy management maintenance service provider to replace its in-house facility management department to deal all related facilities maintenance tasks in warehouse. Then, it is possible that it needs to pay long time facilities maintenance service fee to its outsourcing facility management maintenance service provider more than itself facility management maintenance service provision department.

In conclusion, to decide whether the company ought need or not need facilities maintenance service or either set up in-house facility management department or outsource one facility management maintenance service provider. It depends on whether its organization has how many facilities are used in its workplace, how many staffs are working the workplace, how much size of its workplace, its workplace is office or warehouse or factory, how long time of its facilities' useful time etc. factors , then it can decide whether it needs or does not need one facility maintenance service department or outsourcing facility maintenance service provider to help it to deal any facilities management problem in its organization.

● Facility management role in organization

When one company feels that it has need facility management service. It can choose to set up either in-house facility management department or seek one outsourcing facility management service provider to help it to arrange any facility management service need. However, this facility management role is only one for the organization. It concerns this question: What facility management maintenance function can bring the benefits to the organization?

It can define that all services required for the management of building and real estate to maintain and increase their value, the means of providing maintenance support, project management and user management during the building life cycle, the integration of multi-disciplinary activities within the built environment and the management of their impact upon people and the workplace. In traditional, (FM) services may include building fabric maintenance, decoration and refurbishment, plant, plumbing and drainage maintenance, air conditioning maintenance, lift and escalator maintenance , fire safety alarm and fire fighting system maintenance, minor project management. All these are hard services. Otherwise, cleaning , security, handyman services, waste disposal, recycling, pes control, grounds maintenance, internal plants. All these are soft services. Additional services, might also include: pace planning, things moving management, business risk assessment, business continuity planning, benchmarking, space management, facilities contract outsourcing service arrangement, information systems, telephony, travel booking facility utility management, meeting room arrangement services, catering services, vehicle fleet management, printing service, postal services, archiving , concierge services, reception services, health and safety advice, environmental management.

All of these services will be every organization's in-house facility soft or hard services needs. So, it explains why some large organizations feel need one effective facility management department to help them to arrange how to implement facility services efficiently in order to achieve cost reducing, raising efficiency and performance improvement aims because one effective facility management control system can influence employee individual productive effort to be raised or reduced indirectly.

However, (FM) can be selected either setting up one in-house (FM) department or outsourcing its services to one facility management service provider to help the organization to solve any kinds of facilities maintain service problems. One on-house (FM) department is a team, it needs employees to deliver all (FM) services. Some specialist services are needed to be outsourced, when the service is on expertise in the company. The no expertise services will be outsourced to simple service contracts, e.g. lift and escalator (FM) department will have direct labour, but it can outsource some specialist to help it to do some complex facilities management service. So, the team leader can of can manage whose team staffs, such as maintenance technicians run low risk operations . Otherwise, the outsourcing facility management service provider needs to help it to operate high risk operations or maintenance vital plant facility management service. Anyway, it can set up in-house (FM) department to arrange specialist direct labour and outsourced (FM) services to more than one facility management service providers to do different kinds of (FM) services. One of these outsourcing (FM) service provider, who can arrange sub-contractors to assist it to finish any (FM) services of it's outsourcing (FM) services are more complex to compare the other sub-contractors (third parties).

● What is a facility manager's role to provide quality service to satisfy its user needs?

We need to know how quality can be defined in facility management and why it should be defined by the customer? How facility managers can find out customer (user) needs? What are the difficulties in finding out users' needs and in delivering quality services? Whether improving quality always means requiring higher cost?

In general, facility manager's major responsibilities may include these major functional areas: longer range and annual facility planning, facility financial forecasting, real estate acquisition and/or disposal, work specification, installation and space management, architectural and engineering planning and design, new construction and/or renovation, maintenance and operations management, maintenance and operation management, telecommunications integration, security and general administrative services. When the facility manager had implemented any one of these FM services for those user. How does he/she provide excellent (FM) service quality ot let whose users to feel satisfactory?

In fact, quality issues can not be considered without customer-oriented perspective service quality involves a comparison of expectation with performance. (FM) service quality is a measure of how well to service level delivered matches customer expectation. So, these issues are (FM) service user's general measurement level requirement. The (FM) manager needs to achieve these the minimum performance measurement level to satisfy whose (FM) user's needs.

However, (FM) service quality has three characteristics: Intangibility, heterogeneity, inseparability. But in fact, (FM) service delivered may be through tangible physical aspects, e.g. factory plant workplace building, machine equipment maintenance, intangible (FM) services, e.g. managing space moving in plant to let staffs to work, managing outsourcing cleaners to clean factory equipment. However, all (FM) service performance often varies, due to the behavior of service personnel. Hence, a well developed job specification and training can help to improve the consistence of services of (FM). Any (FM) production and consumption of many services may are inseparable and they are usually interactions between the (FM) client and the contact person from the service provider.

Hence, it seems that service quality is considered as hard to evaluate. In (FM) service quality, it includes physical quality and interactive non-physical service quality. Physical quality is tangibles: The appearance of the physical facilities, equipment, personnel and communication materials. Non-physical services quality means reliability: The ability to perform the promised service dependably and accurately; responsiveness means the willingness to help customers and provide promopt service to let user to feel; assurance mans the competence of the system in its credibility in providing a courteous and secure service and empathy means the approachability, ease of access and effort taken to understand customers' needs.

Hence, a good performance of (FM) manager , he/she ought satisfy the user's tangible and non-tangible both service quality needs. I recommend that he/she can attempt to predict what are the (FM) customer expects in each (FM) service needs. Then, it can make decision what aspect(s) will be the (FM) users major (FM) service need and what aspect(S) won't be the (FM) users major (FM) service need. Then, he/she can make more accurate decision to arrange time, human resource , cost spending amount arrangement whether when it ought concentrate on finishing the (FM) major service tasks as well as whether how he/she ought finish the major (FM) service tasks to be more easily, e.g. how to arrange staffs number to finish, how many the minimum staffs number is needed to be arrange the major (FM) service tasks, time arrangement is important factor, because it can influence whether he/she ought finish the major (FM) service tasks today or tomorrow or later in order to have enough time to finish other non-major (FM) service tasks. Instead of time management, staff number arrangement is also important factor , if he/she arranged the excessive staffs number to do the (FM) major services tasks, then it is possible that it will have shortage of staffs number to finish the non-major (FM) service tasks on the day. So, avoiding either major or non-major (FM) services can not finish on the day. The (FM) manager needs to predict when the major (FM) services and the non-major (FM) services which are necessary to be finished in order to have enough time and staffs to assist him/her to finish every day major and non-major (FM) service effectively. Then, the achievement of his/her (FM) major and non-major tangible and non-tangible services , it will have more chance to be performed efficiently by his/her managed staffs.

In conclusion, in any organizations , (FM) manager needs have good predictable effort to evaluate whether when his/her managed team need to finish the major and/or non-major (FM) tasks as well as whether how he/she ought arrange the accurate time and staff number to finish any major and/or non-major (FM) service tasks on the day. Then, his/her leading of (FM) service team can be managed to work more efficiently in order to satisfy her/his (FM) service user's needs.

How (FM) space moving management
can bring valued add to organizations

There are interesting questions: How (FM) can bring value-add to avoid loss or earn more profit to the organization? Can it influence employees to raise performance and improve efficiency ? Some organizations' (FM) service need which is necessary in order to let employees can raise productivity.

It is based on these assumptions: I assume the organizations have completely either outsourced or in-house their (FM) facility management departments will gain more effect on added value than they have no (FM) function as well as organizations have a strong coordination with the (FM) department will gain more added value than organizations with a weak coordination. Organizations in the profit aim can gain more added value than organizations in the not for profit aim sectors.

In fact, any organization is difficult to confirm it has relationship between improving performance, raising efficiency and owning (FM) function in its organization. (FM) could have to do with the attraction of easy but incomplete indicators of efficiency rather than the necessarily and less direct measures if the effectiveness and the relevance of space moving useful management, e.g. whether building has the enough space to let employees to move to work easy in order to raise efficiency, whether the building has excessive furniture and equipment number and they are putted on wrong places to be caused employees move difficulty in the building in order to influence productive performance.

However, how to arrange space moving management to equipment, e.g. copying machines, faxes, productive machines, they are putted on the locations where have enough space to let employees to move to another locations. For example, the building floor has more than 50 employees, but its space is not enough to let these 50 employees to move to any locations to let them to feel easily often. Then, it is possible to cause they feel nervous pressure and they can feel difficult to work , when they are working in a small office space or factory space or warehouse space. Then, the consequence will be under-predictive efficiency or poor performance to any one of these 50 employees in this office or factory or warehouse.

" Facility management is responsible for coordinating all efforts related to planning, designing, and managing buildings and their systems, equipment, and furniture to enhance. The organizations abilty to compete successfully in a rapidly changing world." (F.Becker)

The author explains equipment, workplace internal space designing, furniture space putting location arrangement will have possible to influence employee individual productive performance or efficiency to be raised or reduced in the workplace. Hence, it seems that, in the value chain (FM) belongs to the activity part of the firm. To make the facilities cooperation with each office or factory or warehouse using space moving facility management. Facility space moving management must be linked strategically, tactically and operationally to other support activity to add value to the organization's office or factory or warehouse space moving management arrangement more effectively.

Thus, how to arrangement space moving management issue it will have possible to influence the organization's employee individual productive performance and efficiency in whose workplace. It seems that (FM) space moving management arrangement have indirect relationship to influence the organization's employee individual performance and efficiency , due to they need often to work in the workplace, if they feel moving difficulty , or excessive equipment , furniture number is putting into the small office, factory or warehouse locations, or they feel the office or factory or warehouse has excessive (a lot of) staffs number to work in the small space of office or factory or warehouse. Then, they can not concentrate nervous on finishing every tasks in possible. In long term, their efficiencies will be poor or inefficiencies or their performance won't be improved or causing poor performance in possible.

Instead of the not enough space moving and excessive staffs number factor, it will bring another question: Can enough information systems equipment cause a more efficient and improved performance to the organization staffs in the workplace?

I assume that the office has 100 employees and it has only ten copying machines. So it means that ten employees use one copying machine. Hence, it brings this question: Is it enough to provide only ten copying machines to average ten employees to use? It depends on other factors, e.g. whether any one of these 100 employees needs to print how many documents per day , whether the five copying machines' locations are far away to separate different locations or they are stored in one printing room in the office, whether the day has how many staffs are absent, whether the day has how many printing machine(s) is/ are broken to need to be repaired. Hence, these unpredictable external environment factors will influence whether the five copying machines number is enough to let these 100 employees to use in the office every day. Hence, facility manager ought need to spend to observe average their copying behaviors every day in order to make data record. Many employees need to use copy machines to print documents, average how many document's page number, they need to print, how much average time spending to print their documents, average how many staff absent number on the day. Even, if the all five copying machines are stored in the printing room, calculating the staffs number whether how many staffs need more than five minutes to walk to the printing room to print their documents many staffs need to spend five minute to walk to the printing room, and they have other urgent tasks to wait to finish. It is possible to influence their efficiency, due to they often need to spend more than five minutes to walk to the printing room to print documents. If there are many staffs need to often to print documents, but their printing task will have many time, e.g. 20 separate printing tasks. Then, they need to spend at least (20x5) 100 minutes to spend time to walk to the printing room to print their documents. It must influence that they should not finish the other urgent tasks on the day. If there are many staffs to spend much time to walk to the printing room in the least 20 separate printing time or more on that day. All the facility manager needs to evaluate whether all the five copy machines are stored in the printing room whether it is the best location decision or they ought need be separated to put on different office locations in their workplaces, even he/she ought need to evaluate whether it is enough copying machines number, when the office has only 5 copying machines. He/she ought need to buy more copying machines number to satisfy any one of these 100 employee individual copying task need.

In conclusion, effective office or factory or warehouse space moving facility management will be one part task of (FM) function. If the office or factory or warehouse can have accurate equipment, machine , furniture number to avoid excessive or shortage number problem to cause employees often feel moving difficult problem in their workplace when they need to move to another location to work in office or warehouse or factory as well as whether the staff needs often spend time to wait the another employee to use the copying machine to print whose document or fax machine to deliver whose document. Then, it is not that fax or printing machines number is not enough to provide the employees to use in the office or warehouse or factory workplace.

Hence, (FM) includes space moving facility management to equipment , machines, furniture number as well as choosing anywhere is(are) the suitable location (s) arrangement to putting or storing these facilities in workplace as well as decision of the staff number and the workplace area size whether it has excessive staffs number to cause these staffs need to work in the small area size of office or warehouse or factory workplace. So, the organization ought need to decide whether it needs to reduce the office's staffs number to let them to work in another more suitable locations in another workplace. Hence, all these facilities space moving management and staffs and workplace size issues will be (FM) manager's consideration issues, because these external environment factors will influence employee individual efficiency and performance to be poor to cause low valued to its organization in long term in possible .

Reference

Becker, F. (1990). " Facility management : a cutting edge field?" property management 8 (2): 25-28.

● Predictive the choosing right
data asset and (FM) analytics
solutions to boost public
transportation service quality , includes airport airplan flying transport service providing organization

Can gather the choosing right data public transportation service station facilities asset and analytics, it can give recommendation to help any organization to boost service quality? (FM) analytics data can be applied to public transportation service industry to be supported how and why the train, train, ferry , ship, air plane, underground train public transportation tools' time arrival and leaving information notice board and automated ticket paying machines facilities are putting on or stored any where locations in order to boost passengers to feel their facilities locations are convenient to let them to buy tickets and see the arrival and leaving time for the next public transportation tool from the information notice electronic board machine. So, it seems that these public transportation tools' station facilities locations can influence passengers to feel the public transportation service company how to consider to its passenger's buying ticket needs and next public transportation tool's arrival and leaving time information needs in order to boost its passengers use service quality and let them to feel better service reliable performance in any train, tram, ferry , ship, underground tram, airplane stations.

As these public transportation service organizations need to learn data analytics represent an opportunity for its ticket paying machine equipment facilities as well as the next transportation tool arrival and leaving time information notice board electronic equipment facilities anywhere the locations are the most suitable to put on or store these equipment to let passengers to walk to the ticket paying machines to buy the ticket to catch the train, tram, underground train, ferry, airplane, taxi, ship more easily. So, they do not need to spend more time to find these facilities locations and spend more time to queue to wait to buy ticket to catch the public transportation tool in stations conveniently. Instead of where is the seeking ticket paying machine location, where is the next public transportation tool arrival and leaving information notice time , these both issues will be any public transportation tool's passenger's main needs.

Hence, how to spend time to seek where the next public transportation tool's arrival and leaving time information electronic notice machine location and where the ticket paying machine location , these both factors will influence any passengers' positive or negative emotion causing. For example, if the passenger feels difficult to find the ticket paying machine in the large area size train station or /and he/she feels difficult to find the train time arrival and leaving information to let him/her to know when the next train will arrive the station. Due to he/she feels difficult to find the train ticket paying machine, he/she needs to spend much time to find any one ticket paying machine in the train station. Then, it will influence him/her to choose another public transportation tool to replace the train public transportation tool, e.g. he/she can choose to catch tram, underground train, taxi, bus, ferry, taxi, ship to replace train. So, it seems ticket paying machine and time arrival and leaving information notice electronic equipment 's location putting or stored choice will be one factor to influence the passenger to choose another kind of public transportation tool to replace train at the moment. When, he/she feels that he/she arrives the destination in the most short time. Then, the public transportation service organization (FM) manager has responsibility to evaluate whether there are enough ticket paying machines number to let passengers do not need to spend more time to queue to buy tickets to catch the public transportation tool in short time as well as there are enough time arrival and leaving for next transportation tool to let passengers to know. It will be their concerning issues when they arrive the public transportation service tool's station.

Hence, predictive passenger individual walking behavior can help the public transportation service organization to choose whether where are the most convenient and attractive locations to let the ticket paying machines and the arrival and leaving time information electronic board machines to be putted on or stored in the suitable station positions in order to let many passengers can find these essential facilities in stations very easily. So, gathering data concerns passenger walking behavior in the public transportation service any stations, which can help the facility manager to make more accurate evaluation to attempt to predict whether where the locations are common places to let passengers to choose to walk daily or where the locations are not common places to let passenger to choose not to walk daily in general. Then, he/she can apply these data of different locations in the stations to evaluate whether anywhere they will have many passengers to choose to walk or whether anywhere they won't have many passengers to choose to walk in order to make more accurate decision whether anywhere are the most suitable locations to let the ticket paying machines and the time arrival and leaving information electronic board equipment to be putter on or stored in order to let them to feel it is so easier to let them to find.

Anyway, calculating each station's passenger number per day issue is important to predict whether where , there are many passengers choose to walk or where, there are not many passengers choose to walk in these different public transportation service stations in order to evaluate whether where the stations' different ought put on paying ticket machines or time arrival and leaving information electronic boards in order to let they feel very easy to buy tickets and seeing the next arrival and leaving time information for the kind of public transportation service tool conveniently in the different stations. Moreover, if the station has no enough ticket paying machines number to be supplied to let passengers need to spend more than ten minute time to wait to buy ticket to catch the kind of public transportation service tool in every queue every day. Then it will cause them to choose another kind of public transportation tool to catch go to working place or entertainment place to replace it to on that day. Then, it will cause these passengers who often do not like to queue in the kind of public transportation service tool's any stations, who will not choose to go to anywhere of this kind of public transportation service tool's any stations again. Hence, in long term this kind of public transportation service tool will lose many passengers. Thus, calculating each station's busy time of passengers number , which can predict when it is the busy time and it can make more accurate decision whether the station has need to increase enough ticket paying machines number in order to bring enough supply number to satisfy passengers' ticket purchase need in the busy time.

In conclusion, gathering above all stations' public transportation service equipment facilities number, storing positions data and every station's passenger walking behavior data, they are necessary to any public transportation tool service industry, because these equipment number and storing locations will influence them to make decisions to choose another kind of public transportation tool to replace it's transportation service if they often feel difficult to find these facilities in its different stations. Thus, it is part of task to facility manager's responsibility if the public transportation service organization expects it won't lose many passengers , due to these external environment factor influence and it also implies cheap ticket price does not guarantee the passengers will choose to catch this kind of public transportation service tool to go to anywhere.

The relationship between facility
management and productive
efficiency, include airport airplan staying and flying service performance improvement

It is one interesting question: Can facility management function bring benefits to raise productive efficiency to organizations? I shall indicate some cases to attempt to explain this possible occurrence chance as below:

● Facility management benefit to office workplace

In private organizations, when the firm has facility management department, whether it can bring efficient administration to influence clerks to work efficiently in office, e.g. reducing administrative time or shorten time to work in administrative processes, in order to achieve minimizing clerk number labor cost. How to design office facilities to let office staffs to feel comfortable to work and reducing their pressure to work. It seems that office working environment will influence office staff individual performance. If the office working environment could improve efficiency and creativity of services to satisfy office workers' comfortable working environment needs. It will reduce every administration manager's working pressure when he/she needs often to find methods to attempt to encourage whose administrative clerks to avoid to waste working time to do some non-major administration tasks.

Hence, how to design or allocate or arrange office any facilities' stored locations or whether how many equipment number is the enough to store in the locations, which will influence office employees' working attitude in order to raise or reduce their administration tasks efficiency indirectly, e.g. the office is clean or dirty, whether office reception has enough information telephone switchboard operation facilities, whether every clerk's table has enough computers number to supply to every to use, whether internet speed is fast or slow in order to let any employees can send and receive email to communicate or download any document from internet in short time, whether data processing and computer system maintenance service supply is enough to be repaired to employees' computers immediately when their computers are broken to wait repair, whether website editing facilities operation whether is enough to link to office every staffs in order to let any office staffs can apply internet to do their tasks conveniently in short time.

Hence, all of these general office equipment facilities whether they are enough supplied and their stored positions anywhere are the suitable to assist any clerks to work conveniently, they will influence every office employee's administrative and productive efficiency indirectly as well as all faxes, copying machines, computers, whether internet linking maintenance service time is short or long to prepare to any office employees to use conveniently any time, these different issues will also influence every employee individual efficiency in office. Hence, it concludes that office working environment, facilities supply number, facilities maintenance service and facilities location storing both factors will influence employee individual administrative productive efficiency in office.

● facility management benefits to service working environment

Can effective facility management improve service working environment to raise employee individual work performance? It is a concern about the quality of service to its customer question. The term" standards and goals" are often used to measure staff individual service performance whether he/she can serve to customers to let them to feel this staff's service performance or attitude is good or bad.

Is the service workplace working environment facilities enough, it will influence customer service staff individual performance.

For shopping center service industry case example, for this situation, e.g. shopping center's facilities are enough or are placed to the suitable locations in order to let the shopping center's customers to feel comfortable to shopping when they enter this shopping center as well as whether the shopping center's facilities can influence the customer service staffs to serve whose shopping customers easily or difficult, due to whether the shopping center's facilities whether are adequate supplied or their locations are the best suitable positions to influence their service performance to let them to feel easier or comfortable to serve their customers in any large size shopping centers. For example, whether the lamps' lighting energy is enough to let the shoppers to feel safe to walk to visit any shops when there are many shoppers were walking to cause crowd and they feel difficult to walk to avoid any body contact to any one in busy time when the shopping center has no enough lights to let them to see anywhere in the shopping center's dark environment. Then it will influence customer service staffs to feel difficult to find any shopping center customers, e.g. when two shopping center customers are fighting in one location where is far away to the shopping customer service staffs and securities in the shopping center, because the shopping center is large and it has no enough light to let the customer service staffs and securities to find their frighting location to deal their fighting behavior and other shopping center's shoppers will feel very dangerous to walk their fighting location to avoid to close them. Then, it will has possible to cause death or hurt to any one of these two fighting shoppers ,even other shoppers' life. Because the shopping center's securities and customer service staffs who need to spend much time to find their fighting location, it will delay they can bring the policemen to their fighting location when they arrive this shopping center's destination in short time in order to solve their fighting behavior to influence all shoppers' life in this shopping center. Hence, the shopping center whether it has enough lamps number and the lamps' light whether is enough, these lighting facilities will influence any shopping center customer service staffs and securities who can spend less time to arrive any locations to deal any urgent matters.

For another situation in shopping center, if the shopping center has no enough paying telephone service facilities to supply shoppers to phone to anyone when they feel need to phone to any in the shopping center. Then, it will lead to some shoppers decide to find where the shopping center's reception's telephone to supply to them to phone call to anyone. If they are ten shoppers are waiting to use the shopping center's reception telephone to phone call to their friend or family within one minute. Thus, it will influence the reception customer service staffs feel difficult to arrange how to distribute the only one telephone to these ten shoppers to use to phone call their friend or family when they are queuing within their one minute waiting time in the shopping center's reception. If these ten shoppers can not use the reception telephone to phone call anyone. hen, they will feel dissatisfactory and complain to the reception service staffs politely. So, lacking enough facilities in the shopping center's any where, it will possible to influence their shopping centers' shoppers to feel all shopping center's service staff individual performance to be poor. It means that if the shopping center expects to improve customer satisfaction to its customer service staff's behavioral performance, it meets have enough facilities to be supplied in the shopping center to let its shoppers to feel it is one comfortable and safe shopping center. In conclusion, shopping center's facilities will have possible to influence shoppers' feeling to evaluate its customer service staffs to evaluate whether their service attitudes are good or poor indirectly.

● Can facility management improve productivity

The productivity means resources (input) is therefore the amount of products or services (output), which is produced by them. Hence, higher (improved) productivity means that more is produced with the same expectation of resource, i.e. at the same cost is terms of land materials, machine, time or labor. Alternatively, it means same amount is produced at less labor cost in term of land, material, machine, time for labor that is utilized. So, it brings this question: How can facility management improve productivity? I shall explain as these several aspects, it is possible to be improved productivity from (FM) successfully.

Improved productivity of farm land: If the farming land has better facility management to bring advantages by using better seed, better facilities of cultivation and most fertilizer. It is in the agricultural sense is increased (

improved). So, facility management can bring benefits to any land resource to raise productivity in possible. It implies that the productivity of land used for better facility management of industrial purposes is said to have been increased if the output of products or service within that area of industrial land is increased output aim.

Improved productivity of material: If the factory has improved better equipment by facility management method to assist skillful workers to raise the manufacture cloth number, then the productivity of the cloth number is improved by (FM) method.

Improved productivity of labour: When the factory has good manufacturing equipment facilities to be supplied to improve methods of work to product more producing number per hour, then (FM) improved productivity of worker. Hence, in any workplaces, when organization has good facilities, it will influence employees to raise productivities in possible, because they need often to improved equipment facilities manufacture products to achieve higher production number aim.

● Can facility management raise bank employee
productivity, include airport employee service performance improvement

Bank workplace environment is busy, the bank counter service staffs need to contact many bank clients to help them to serve or withdraw money from bank's counters. Whether does the quality of environment in bank workplace will influence the determination level of employee's motivation, subsequent performance productivity in bank working environment. For example, if the bank's staffs need work under inconvenient conditions , it will bring low performance and face occupational health diseases causing high absenteeism and turnover.

In general, bank size is usually small, it will have many bank clients enter bank to contact counter staffs to need them to help them to save or withdraw money. So, it will bring air pollution the crowd queue in every bank counter challenge when the bank has many people are queue waiting in counters to queue. So, bank working condition problem relates to environmental and physical factors which will influence every bank counter staff individual working performance to serve bank clients satisfactory. However, bank staffs need to deal many documents concern every client personal data every day. So, they need to spend much time to use computer and painting machines. This is particularly true for these employees who spend most of the day operating a computer terminal in bank workplace. As more and more computers are being installed in workplaces, an increasing number of business has been adopting designs for bank offices installment. So, bank needs have effective facilities management design because of demand of bank staffs for more human comfort.

An good equipment facility management for bank staffs to use conveniently, it is assumed that better workplace environment can motives bank employees and produces better productivity. Hence, bank office environment can be described in terms of physical and behavioral components to influence bank staffs to work inefficiently. To achieve high level of bank employee productivity, bank organizations must ensure that the physical environment in conductive to bank different department organizational needs, facilitating interaction and privacy, formality and informality, functional and disciplinarily, e.g. house loan or private loan departments, counter service department, visa card application department.

Thus, in a high safe privacy facility management working environment will let different department bank staffs feel safe to worry about privacy loss in possible. So, the improving bank facility to bring safe and high privacy to avoid bank client individual loss in working environment issue, the facility management can be results to bring these benefits, such as in a reduction in a number of complaints and absenteeism and an increase in productivity.

● Can (FM) create value to organization?

(FM) can reduce managing facilities as a strategic resource to add value to the organization and its overall performance, e.g. saving the energy in building and take care of shuttle buses and parking facilities space management for , on economic efficiency and effectiveness, or good price and value for the organization.

If the organization expects to apply (FM) process to save energy, it depends on possible input factors, i.e. interventions in the accommodation facilities services. So, it seems that the organization expects to save its energy consumption in its building. It needs have good space management facilities between parking its shuttle buses in its property's car park.

Why does space facility management is important to influence efficiency and productivity. For one school's building example, when the school decides none of the two gymnasiums student sport entertainment centers to be built in order to reduce financial cost and higher benefits. Remarkably, the use of space with the school overall strategic goals , such as creating spaces that better can support the teaching, motivate students and teachers, attract more students and increase the utilisation of existing space to accommodate an increasing number of students.

If it hopes to make high quality teaching facilities on student's choice where to study. The school will need to choose to build either one comfortable and new design facility teaching accommodation or build two gymnasium sport entertainment centers in its limited land space either for students' learning or sport aim. Due to it feels new teaching accommodation can make more attractive to increase students numbers to choose it to study more than building two new gym sport centers to let them do sport in school.

Hence, space choice (FC) management strategy will be one important considerable issue, when the organization has limited land space resources to make choose to build any constructions in order to increase many clients number. Such as the school organization has limited storage land resource to let it to build either two gymnasium sport entertainment centers or one new teaching accommodation in order to attract many students to choose it to learn. Hence, it needs to gather data to make more accurate evaluation to decide how to apply its space facility to choose to build these both kinds of buildings in order to achieve the attractive student learning choice aim, so whether the two sport entertainment activity centers or one new teaching accommodation choice, it needs to gather information to decide whether the school ought to choose to build which kind of building in order to achieve the increase of student number aim, so space facility management will be this school's land shortage problem.

The relationship between facility
management and consumer
behavior, include airport travel passenger service satisfactory feeling

How and why shop facility management can influence consumer individual shopping behavior? If it is possible, what shop facility management factors can influence their consumption decision when they enter the shop to plan to buy anything. I shall indicate some shop case studied to explain whether how and why every shop's facility management can influence consumer individual consumption desire when any one consumer enters any shops.

● Shop's low ceiling height location (FM) influence consumer behavior
Can the shop's ceiling height influence shoppers' shopping behavior? Can the shop's variation in ceiling height can influence how consumers process information to decide to make purchase decision in the shops, e.g. for this

situation, when the consumer enters the shop, he/she feels the ceiling height is low and it has a lamp will contact his/her head in possible. So, he/she chooses to move far away from the low ceiling location in the shop. It is possible that shop's ceiling low height and the lamp locates at the ceiling low height position will influence many customers' choices to leave the low ceiling height and lamp location, then the shop's low ceiling height will have possible to influenced many customers to choose to find the another shop to buy the similar kind of products , due to the lamp locates in the low ceiling height, so this lamp and low ceiling height will be possible factor to influence any shoppers who won't choose to walk to this dangerous location in the shop. If the shop's all spaces are ceiling height and it has many lamps are located at the low ceiling height spaces. Then, it will be serious to cause many shoppers do not want to spend too much time to choose any products in the shop because they feel dangerous to walk to the any low ceiling height lamps' locations in the shop.

Hence, hoe to design the different concept may be activated by the showroom ceiling if it were relatively high, as it tends to be in mall stores, versus low, as it is in most strip mall shops and outlet centers. Relatively high ceilings may bring safe shopping emotion to let any consumers to feel thoughts related to freedom, whereas lower ceilings may let consumers to feel dangerous to walk the locations in any shops. Hence it seems any shops ought not neglect whether their ceiling height is tall and the lamps ought avoid to locate in any low ceiling height locations in order to influence consumers number to be decreased.

● Can house facility management influence consumer individual purchase intention?

When one new property is built, whether the property consumers will consider how the new property is facility to influence their purchase intention to the property will the new property's (FM) influence buyers in real estate markets' preferences choice and living interest. Any new property's internal characteristics of the house unit itself , such as rooms available, when example, of external are location, accessibility to utilities services and facilities will have possible to influence the property buyer's final property purchase decision, so it seems that even the property price is cheap, it is not represent the property buyer will choose to buy the property, if he/she feels the property's facility management is poorer to compare other similar kinds of properties.

So, it can help real estate analysts better explain and predict the behavior of decision makers in real estate markets. Property consumers will search for property information, concerns the property's quality, price distinctiveness, ability, facility management, service of the property's external environment to decide whether the property is high value to choose to buy to compare other kinds of properties.

However, the external environmental forces, such as limited resources, e.g. time or financial will influence whose property consumption choice and living the property's satisfaction feeling (represent) a feedback from post-property purchase reflection used to inform subsequent decisions. The process of the property buyer's leaving experience will serve to influence the extent to which the property consumer how to consider future next time property purchases decision and new information methods. Hence, when one property consumer chooses to buy a house, it refers house features are house internal attributes , such as quality of building, the design as well as internal and external design, which are important factors for a property consumer when he/she needs to select and purchases one house.

The other (FM) factors which can influence the property consumers' needs, include living space as features, such as the size of kitchen, bathroom, bedroom, living bath and other rooms available in the house. The environment of housing area is also important factor, e.g. the condition of the hood, attractiveness of the area, quality of houses, type of houses, type of houses, density of housing, wooded area or free coverage, slope of the attractive views, open space, non-residential uses in the areas vacant sites, traffic noise, level of owner-occupation in , level of education in level of income in, security from crime, quality of schools, religious of , transportation , shopping center, sport entertainment can be supplied to close to the house area. All these human related issue of the property's location will also influence the property buyer's living location selection. Hence, above (FM) influence property consumer purchase behavior, it is based on the relationship behavior. The consumer's house purchase intention and house features, living space, environment and distance to recreation center, supermarket, library etc. public facilities variable (FM) factors.

In conclusion, the house internal space facility management and external environment facility management factors will influence property consumer individual house purchase intention.

● The effects of in-store shelf design facility management factor influences consumer behavior

Can every store retailer's shelf design influence supermarket and large retail stores shoppers' behaviors when they visit the stores? However, currently many stores tend to build on traditional and repetitive design for their store shelf layout, it brings results in outdated store layouts.

Another important store shelf layout design aspect, retailer should consider carefully is the allocation of products on shelves. So, it seems that efficient shelf space allocation management does not only minimize the economic threats of empty product shelves, it can also lead to higher consumer satisfaction, a better customer relationship.

Why does supermarket shelves design is important? Any retail tore will sell product category within a shelf. They can use the same nominal category , e.g. crisps next to light crisps, same food product shelf. Anyway, a goal-based shelf display can contain several product, that determine a common consumer goal, e.g. fair trade. Hence, these two categorical product structuring methods are also described in terms of how to put product, or food on shelf benefit and attribute -based product categories.

These shelf design food or product storing method will have more influence consumers to choose to buy the supermarket or retail store food or products more easily , due to products, or food put on their shelf very convenient and systematic to attract consumers' shopping consideration to the supermarket or retail store.

● Music (FM) environment influence consumer consumption desire

Is it possible that shop music (FM) environment can raise consumer purchase desire? In one shop or supermarket, it can provide soft music (FM) equipment to let consumers can listen soft music or songs in the supermarket or retail shop when the are staying to spend more time shopping and whether soft music facility can be expected to raise customer individual value-added options to the music facility shop in the supermarket or retail shop.

Can the music facilities prolong consumers to stay in the store? It is possible that tempo soft music can influence consumers to stay longer time in restaurants and supermarkets and retail shops. It is possible that the different types of music (FM) in any supermarket, restaurant, retail shop owning music listening facility shopping environment. It will have possible to influence consumers to prolong staying in their shops. For example, one wine selling retail shop has classical music (FM) listening equipment to let consumers to listen when they enter the wine shop, it is possible to cause consumers to choose to buy more expensive wine products. Some researchers indicate when the wine shop owns classical music facility to let all consumers can list classical music when they walk in the wine ship, it can evoke the wine consumers to choose to buy purchasing higher prices wine products in the long term classical music listening environment. Otherwise, in a fitness sport center, musical fir and excite or popular music (FM) environment can attract fitness sport players' emotion to play and kind of fitness sport facility longer time. Also, in one supermarket, the soft music facilities listening environment can persuade or attract food consumers to spend more time in the mall consuming food or beverage also purchase other products more easily, due to they will listen soft music to be influenced to choose to prolong staying time in the supermarket. It seems that it has relationship between retail shop's music facility environment and consumer's emotion will be influenced by these different kinds of soft music or songs to raise consumption desire in the supermarket, if some consumers like to prolong to stay longer consuming time in the owning music facility environment's retail shop.

In fact, some researchers indicate the owning background music facility selling environment's ship , it can affect consumer decision making, memory, concentration consumption desire. So, classical , jazz soft music facility ought be installed in restaurants, retail shops, restaurants' environment. Otherwise, popular , exciting, noise, pop music facility ought be installed in fitness sport centers, theme park entertainment parks business places in order to influence fitness sport players or theme park entertainers to prolong playing or entertaining time to feel real sport or entertainment theme park playing machine facility's entertainment enjoyable feeling as well as attracting restaurant or supermarket or retail shop's consumers to prolong their staying time to make consumption decisions. Hence, it seems that music facility environment can raise consumers' consumption desire in possible.

● University bookstore atmospheric factors how to influence student's purchase book behavior?

Any university bookstore how to do international control and structuring of book internal environment to raise students' purchase book desires in university itself school's bookstore, it will be one popular question to any universities. Hence, whether the university bookstore internal (FM) factors include: lighting, music, colors, scents, temperature, layout and general cleanliness as well as university external factors include: the university bookstore shape/size, windows, university parking facility for students availability and location, which can play an influential role of the university bookstore image in order to influence the university itself students to choose to buy books from themselves bookstore or university outside bookstores.

Whether the university student needs to spend how long individual learning time and how much learning nervous to spend time to choose any kinds of book in the universiity bookstore or outside bookstores, this issue , he/she will consider. Because he/she does want to expect spend much time and nervous to choose to buy books in any bookstore. If the university's bookstore physical location and internal (FM) image can let its target student customers to feel it's all book products are stored in any attractive internal book shelves places, e.g. the cheapest and the most expensive different subjects of text books are stored in one system method to bring the positive image of value and quality in order to let university target student customers can find their books' choice location to spend less time to search any books to read in the unviersiity bookstore easily.

However, due to learning time is shortage to every university student of the university's book shelves can display all text books in the attractive right locations in the university bookstore as well as the university's bookstore ought has an adequate space to let university students to walk to anywhere and find any subjects of text books and compare their book sale prices in the bookstore's any shelves' locations easily when they walk to the subject of book shelf location, then they can make accurate decision either to buy the right kind of subject book or not buy it to read in the short time. They will feel their book choice purchase decision making process won't influence their learning time in themselves universiity. Then, the university students will be influenced by themselves university's bookstore's attractive external university facilities in the university's any teaching places and the university's bookstore internal attractive environment facility image which can influence the students to make final choices to buy their liking books to read from their university's itself bookstore. Hence, the university's bookstore internal and external building environment (FM) design factors will influence its students whether choose to buy from themselves bookstore or another outside general bookstore.

● How and why does retail atmospheric environment influence consumers behavior in retail shop?

Any shop's internal facility management design can influence atmospheric environment to influence consumer individual shopping desire, e.g. colour, lighting, music, crowding, design and layout factors, which internal shop (FM) environment can influence the first time shopping visiting client ' cognitive process how to feel the shop store image. Such as if the store's (FM) environment can bring enjoyable and fun and happy image to let them to feel shopping's enjoyment.

In conclusion, when consumers will like to stay longer time in the store. Due to the store's internal (FM) atmospheric environment can attract them to stay longer time in the store. Then, the customer's shopping value will raise and it can bring purchasing intention and shopping satisfaction. How can (FM) influence retail atmospheric physical (FM) environment ? Can (FM) bring indirect relationship to influence how the consumer individual causes positive or negative purchase intention when he/she has influence to prolong staying desire in the store, when the shop has good (FM) , it will bring long time to make consumption chance in the shop.

● Facility management influences

consumer satisfactory service

level, include airport travel passenger satisfactory service performance level

Can facility management (FM) quality influence consumer satisfactory service feeling? Any organization's facility management can improve the effectiveness of the maintenance organization. It can provide improved operational and maintenance functions to maintain the physical environment to support the overall mission. However, any organization will consider whether it improves its facilities, it will raise consumer satisfactory feeling when it provides the service to them, e.g. education service industry, when students need to often to attend any school's classrooms or lecture halls, computer rooms, libraries, all these facilities will be student's learning environment. If these school facilities can be maintenance to let students to feel comfortable to enjoy to study in their schools' any learning locations. Then, it has possible that to bring their enjoyable learning feeling in theirs schools.

● How school's facility management influences student's learning satisfactory feeling.

However, in education industry case, the school's facility management has those criteria can be used to measure effectiveness. Student individual response time between the student's request for computer use service in school computer rooms, library reading service in school library , classroom computer facilities and tables, chairs etc. furniture supplies service and the facility management supply number and available to useful time. If the student believes that the response time is too long when he/she feels need to use any school facilities, the actual number of seconds or minutes, he/she needs to wait how long time to queue to use his/her school's any facilities in library, classroom, computer room. So, the student's queue waiting time to use any his/her school's facilities, it can measure the school's facility management effectiveness.

● Scheduling of preventive maintenance activities.

It schedules of any maintenance activities are not arranged effectively to the school. Then, it will influence students' poor learning facility service to their school. For their situation, when the school's first floor has two men toilets are damaged. They are needed to be required. However, it is one week period, the first floor 100 students can not use the first floor men toilets. Hence, in this week, all 100 students need to go to other floors toilets to often use. They will feel busy and time is not enough when they need to attend to any classrooms to listen the first floor classrooms teachers' lesson. If he/she arrives the first floor classroom too late, due to he/she needs to go to another floor male toilets to queue to use. Then, he/she will feel angry and worries about whose absent or late attending classroom behavior when the lesson's teacher has attended early in the first floor classroom , and he teacher will need him/her to explain why he/she will go to this classroom lately, if his/her explanation won't be accepted to attend to the first floor classroom too late in the week. So, arrangement maintenance schedule to any school's facilities issue is importnt to influence student's satisfactory feeling to the school. Also, lacking of preventive maintenance activities will bring results in unscheduled shutdown of critical equipment can have an unrecoverable impact on the school's good learning environment providing to student's mission.

In fact, however in any organizations, such as school, ship, office etc. organizations, achieving balance of effectiveness and efficient difficulties and takes time and effort on the part of management and staff. It is not enough to establish an optimal relationship between these two parts. It has another factor that organizations need to consider costs. In today's budget tightening environment, decreasing expenses requires accepting a lower level of efficiency and effectiveness. The goal is to determine the point at which decreasing efficiency and effectiveness is no longer acceptable before that point is reached.

It brings this question : How to apply facility management knowledge to rise efficiency and effectiveness in order to improve quality standard of service to satisfy consumers' needs in short time? Such as school's facilities service case. What factors can influence student's level of satisfaction with regards to higher educational facilities services? It seems that any school's facilities will influence its students how to satisfy its education service indirectly. Because they need often to go to school to learn. So, any school's facilities, e.g. classrooms, computer rooms, libraries, toilets, lecture halls, canteens, sport and entertainment centers, research laboratories, school car parks, student enquiry counters, all these places to the school's any students will attend. So, how raise schools' facilities improvement to satisfy students' learning needs in the school's any locations which will have help to influence it student individual satisfaction level to the school's service, instead of every teacher individual teaching performance service to the school's students.

For any service organizations , such as hotels, restaurant, financial institutions, retail stores and hospitals etc. The physical environment can influence how customers' evaluation of their service. Due to service has intangible nature, so customers will rely on evaluate service quality.

Any higher education institutions are education service providing organizations. They need have comfortable and enjoyable educational environment to be provided to the students to attend the school's any places in order to meet whose learning expectations and studying experience needs. So, the school's facility management will be one factor to influence student's learning satisfaction when they expect to attend the school's any locations or places to let them to feel the school's learning environment have good facility management feeling.

In fact, if the school has comfortable classrooms or lecture halls educational environment to let its students to feel, it will bring assistance to raise their learning satisfactory feeling. So, comfortable learning facility management environment is one kind of school's facility service characteristics, it includes intangibility, perishability, inseparability and variability. So, they are every student individual learning feeling when they are attending to the school's any learning locations. So, school's facility management service feeling will influence whether they expect to choose this school to study. If the school's facility management learning environment is more comfortable and teaching facilities are better to compare other schools' facilities. Then, it will have possible to attract many students to choose this school to study. Such as any educational organizations, instead of the teachers (lecturers and professors) whose educational level is influence students number. The university's building environment will influence students' learning feeling, when they attend in the university. The facilities include laboratories, lecture theatres an offices, but also residential accommodations, catering facilities, sports and recreations centers because university students need have university life feeling to let them to fell the university can give welfare services , e.g. medical services, career guidance, sport entertainment, residential accommodation etc. service, instead of educational learning service in classrooms and lecture theatres. Hence, university's diversification facilities services are needed to satisfy university students to choose it to study, instead of university teacher's educational performance. When one student can enroll the university to study from secondary education institution. The admitted student will usually consider two aspects to decide to choose the university to study. One aspect is the academic programs, of sequence of courses choices and the another aspect is the university's facilities whether they can satisfy their university life need, e.g. library, dorms, bookstore, food canteen , gym's sport entertainment, education technological facilities in the classrooms and lecture theatres to let the students to feel the university's teaching facilities are achieved his/her learning demand.

So, these two factors (teaching and learning and facilities) are linked to each other to influence student's total school learning experience and attitude towards a particular institution and this is termed as value chain in the student's learning process in the university. Hence, student individual evaluation variables will include teaching staff, teaching method, enrolment and facility enough supply actual service need.

However, the university's facilities, such as any residential accommodation, canteen, library , classroom, lecture theatre, sport gym, entertainment center will be their useful facilities need to satisfy their learning, entertainment and eating ,even living need in residential accommodation in the school's learning life experience every day. If one student chooses to live in the university residential accommodation . All of his/her learning and eating and living time and spending will be calculated to the university's any facilities to let him/her to feel it can provide enough facilities to let him/her to enjoy.

Hence, the facility management factor, such as overall campus environment, library, laboratory, classroom, lecturer theatre size and facility supply of on campus accommodation, welfare right service, parking areas, cafeteria , sport center etc. They will be every students facilities service needs from the university supplies choice. So, any university ought not neglect how to improve itself university's space area facilities to achieve satisfy their needs after they choose this university to study. Hence, any university's facility management will influence how the student's satisfactory learning service feeling when he/she chooses the university to study.

In conclusion, better facility management will attract more students to choose the university to study. Otherwise, worse facility management will not attract more students to choose to study the school. Hence, it seems that the school's facility management factor has relationship to influence student's satisfactory feeling, instead of teacher individual teaching performance factor to the school.

● Property facility management influences householder buying behavior

One new property's low price is attractive factor to influence property buyer individual preference choice. Does the new individual's facility management factor influence the property buyer's preference choice decision, if the property buyer feels its facility management is better than other similar properties, even it's price is higher than other properties. I shall indicate some cases to analyze this possibility as below:

Some properties' facility management service quality has possible to create true value for any property buyers when they consider the calculation ingredients to make decision whether to new property has higher value to choose to buy. The factors may include: price, natural environment, transportation tools convenient available, shopping centers supplies, the neighour quality, and the property's internal facility management etc. factors.

In fact, car or house purchase buyers, they have similar behaviors. It is that car's buyers will consider the car's machines whether they are safe to drive on roads, instead price, manufacture loyalty factors. It is possible that the car's machines quality factor will be preference to any car buyers when they make preference decisions to choose which brand its cars are the suitable. However, if the car's brand is famous and its appearance beautiful and price is cheap. But the car consumer feels its machine qualities are unsafe to let the driver to drive on road. Then, the car's poor machine quality factor will influence the car buyer's decisions to choose to buy this car. It can influence the car buyer individual car purchase decision.

The car buyer's behavior is similar to property buyer's behavior. Although, the new property price is cheap, good neigh ours are living near to the new property's location, shopping centers and transportation tools are available to near to this new property's area. But if the property buyers' feels its facility management is poor quality to compare other similar properties. Then, the poor quality of facility management factor will have possible to influence the property buyers whose final buying decision to choose to buy this new property. It brings this question: How and why can the facility management poor quality factor influence property consumers' preference choice?

In general, all property consumers won't know whether the new property's facility management is good or bad quality , they need to spend time to visit to the new property in order to observe whether its internal facility is satisfactory to his/her acceptable level. In simple, their purchase decision will regard to how to allocate household budget, how the household's economic resources are influenced, e.g. for travelling, visits to restaurants, comparing the different similar types of property product groups, e.g. apartments or houses or houses of a givn size data. For example, if one property's room(s) size is (re) small to compare other kind similar product type of room(s) size. Although the prior property's price is cheaper to compare to the later properties. But, if some property buyers hoped the property has large room(s) size, then the later larger room(s) size which will be possible to some property buyer's preference choice. Even, their property price is more expensive to compare the smaller room(s) size of properties. Thus, the property's room size which will be one major factor to influence property buyers' purchase decision. room's size had relationship to facility management issue. Moreover, if the room's quality and design is attractive, then it will bring more attractive to persuade some property buyers to choose to buy them to live in preference.

Hence, whether the new property is good durable product feeling which will influence householder's choice. If the householder feels the new property has long term durable life to avoid to spend much maintenance expense when they have been living in the new property for a long term period. They will believe it has better facility management, quality to let them to live longer time and the most importance is that they do not need to spend any maintenance expense , due to the property 's any internal facilities are damaged easily.

The external factors may include: culture, reference groups, family, social class and demography of lifestyle as well as internal factors may include: feelings, past property buying and living experience , property knowledge, motivation of the property buyer individual psychology. These both factors can influence any property buyer individual decision making process to do final house purchase behavior. However, internal factors, such as: property knowledge of facility management and property living experience, e.g. how to evaluate to choose to buy the property , due to the property buyer's past living experience for the past property's facilities whether its facilities can satisfy its property buyers' comfortable living needs. This internal factor will be more important to influence any property buyer's property purchase final decision. If he/she feels whose prior old property's facilities are satisfactory. Then, he/she will compare this new property and old property's facilities to decide whether this new property is value to buy. So, the old property's facility will be the measurement standard to compare his/her next new property purchase choice. So, the property purchaser will compare these new and old property's property facilities product knowledge to similarities among property alternative which will influence his/her final decision to choose to buy the new property to live.

It seems that property low price factor must not guarantee to attractive many property buyers' choice. Otherwise, it is assumed that many property buyers like rent or buy to live the property for themselves for long term intention. There are less property buyers expect to sell the first property to earn profit intention. So, they will usually consider whether the property is long term durable product to avoid to pay maintenance expense when they had been living in the property in long term.

Some factors that taking consideration are proximity to the specific location, housing prices, developer's brand, the payment scheme, reference group, which are not the main factors to influence any property buyer individual choice. Because property buyer's need is that the property has good facilities to supply to them to live, e.g. good heater equipment can provide hot water to them to bath in winter or good air conditioners can provide cold temperature to let them to feel cool comfortable feeling in summer in their homes. Good electric tools facilities , when they have need to use electricity in safe environment at home, e.g. car park accessibility facility , level of security facility , surface area facility and housing types, bedroom, bathroom facilities, quality of housing manufacturing raw material, house design , house durable guarantee, speed of complaint responsiveness, specification accuracy, confirmation of building plan service, showing legal file property purchase process service, finance instalments process assistance, speed of responsiveness, officers' skills of presentation. All of above these concern property facility management issues will influence any property buyers' final choice to decide whether the property is value to buy. So, facility management will influence property purchaser individual final decision in possible.

● Hotel facilities influence hotel consumer choice

Travellers choose hotel to live. They will consider price, room comfortable feeling, hotel location , gum sport or entertainment service facility supplies , hotel room booking service etc. factors to decide whether the hotel can achieve every traveller individual minimum living need. However, whether hotel facilities factor will be the main factor to influence travellers' living needs. How and why do travellers consider hotel facilities whether are enough supply or facilities of quality to satisfy their demand to cause their living choice to the hotel final decision.

Usually, hotel's customers won't plan to live too long time, e.g. more than three months in the hotel. Because they are travelling aim. It will bring this question: Does hotel facilities quality consider to influence their hotel living choice if the traveller is short-term traveller to the country? However , some travellers who have effort to spend money to live high class hotels, even their journey is short trip. Hence it seems that short trip , hotel living reason can not influence the high class hotel travellers' living comfortable demand to the high class hotel room. Hence , the high class hotel room's facility management quality is also needed high performance. Even, when they need to eat breakfast, lunch , dinner in the high class hotel canteens or playing any sport equipment, or gum equipment or wathching movie in the hotel's small cinema room . They must need high class hotel can supply more entertainment, restaurant , sport facilities to satisfy their comfortable needs in the high class hotel. Moreover, they must consider safety issue when they are living in the high class hotel. So, thy must demand the hotel have enough five fright equipment in their rooms, or corridors and the stairs to let them can leave the dangerous locations to arrive the most safe locations immediately when the hotel has fire accident occurrence in any where . So, it ensures that the high class hotel's customers must ensure the high class hotel's facilities can satisfy their any one of above these needs before they decide to live this high class hotel.

In fact, high class hotel's room price must be more expensive to compare the low class hotel. So, it explains why high class hotel's consumers will need the hotel has safe and good quality of facilities to let them to feel it is one reasonable price, safe , good service and good facilities' high class hotel to live. Usually, when the traveller arrives the country to travel, the travelers chooses the hotel to live, it is whose first time visit in common. So, he/she ought consider that the hotel environment seems it is good or bad to let the traveller to select to live. If the hotel's facility environment is new and beauty and design colorful to let the first time travellers to feel. Then, it is possible that good facilities environment can influence the first time travellers to select to live, even the hotel's room price is more expensive to compare other similar hotels in the travelling living places. Hence, it explains why hotel facilities can influence traveller individual room booking choice. When he/she is the first time to visit the hotel to select whether to live or not.

● How and why facility management can influence workplace productivity to bring customer satisfaction

Facility management is one part of manufacturers or retailers as their productivity in workplace as their input and functionalistics within physical environment. In fact, facility management in workplace may include: site selection, property disposal, site acquisition, workplace space allocation, space inventory, space forecasting facility management, interior furniture change planning, interior furniture installation, moving maintenance, inventory, design evaluation, employment satisfaction evaluation plan, external maintenance and breakdown maintenance, preventive maintenance, landscape maintenance, energy space facility management, hazardous waste disposal, capital , operating furniture budgeting. So, it seems that one workplace considered whether the workplace's facility is enough to let employees to work in order to raise efficiency and improve productive performance more easily. Then, it will bring this question:

● How and why workplace facility management can influence consumer individual satisfaction?

Strategic FM delivery is essential for business survival. I shall explain why for delivery is important to influence customer satisfaction. In business process view point, an effective and meaningful service to their customer , i.e. the user. For logistic industry, the product's delivery time will influence when the product can be sent to the user's arrival destination. If the product is delayed to sent to the user's home or office or any location destination. The reason is because the logistic product sender has no efficient facility management (FM) arrangement in its warehouse . Then, its warehouse lacks efficient (FM), which will cause users to feel its delivery service is poor and they will complain its delivery service staffs. Then, they will find another delivery service company to replace its service. So, it explains that logistic industry's warehouse (FM) service arrangement can raise efficient time to send any products to their customers in order to let they feel satisfactory service. For example, Amazon online logistic company's warehouse has applied artificial intelligence robotic tools to assist warehouse workers to arrange the different kinds of products to deliver to the right shelves . Then, the warehouse robotics will follow their right product shelves locations to follow the right products to deliver to US domestic or overseas product buyers in the short time and it can avoid the wrong products to deliver to the wrong buyers' risk. Also, the (AI) delivery tools can raise time efficiency to assist Amazon warehouse workers to reduce their work load, and tried to work in large warehouse environment. Although, its warehouse's area is large, the (AI) tools facility can help them to deliver the different products to different shelves in the right locations , e.g. exact product number and the kinds of product to be delivered to the right country' client's shelf location in the warehouse. Also, it implies FM is very important to influence Amazon warehouse delivery efficiency and avoiding delivery wrong occurrence chance. For example, the shelf location belongs to US domestic customers, or the shelf location belongs to Japan customers, or the shelf location belongs to Hong Kong customers, or any other Asia or Western countries' different customers' locations. The warehouse's facility needs have different countries' shelves enough space to put and it also need enough space to let the (AI) tools, robotic delivery workers and human workers both to walk to different shelves locations easily and the different countries' shelves number needs to be calculated accurate. For example, it has how many client number will buy Amazon's the kind product per day. If it has above 5,000 to 10,000 China clients to buy the kind of product. Then, it will need to make judgement how many shelves are placed in the warehouse. So, it can avoid to lack enough shelves to put any different kinds of products to prepare to delivery to China clients in efficient time and it won't avoid to delay to deliver to their homes or offices or any locations in China.

Hence, such as Amazon logistic case, it explains why warehouse's space shelves number and area or locations facility management can influence workers or (AI) delivery tools how to move convenient and avoiding the delivery to the customer's wrong destination chance occurrence and shortening time to deliver products to its clients efficiently. Then, due to the delivering time is shorten and the wrong delivery destination's occurrence chance is also reduced , even it can avoid to deliver the product to wrong client's destination occurrence. Then, the logistic firm's clients will feel more satisfactory to its product sale delivery service and their complaints will be avoided. Hence, it explains effective warehouse (FM) space management service arrangement is essential to any logistic businesses nowadays.

● Facility management brings departmental benefits

Why do organizations need have facility management (FM) service? As above examples indicate that (FM) can improve workplace environment facilities, e.g. warehouse environment to let workers to raise efficiencies or improve performances, even it can influence consumers to raise satisfactory to it's services indirectly, also it can help organizations' equipment to be used long term to cause old and are needed to spend expenditure to maintenance or change new equipment in order to improve better quality . So , it can assist organizations to avoid to spend more expenditure for new equipment purchase or maintenance. All these issues will be facility management service's benefits to an organizations, which can concern raising customers' service satisfaction, raising efficiency or improving productive performance, raising productivity, reducing equipment or property maintenance or new alternation much of expenditure spending, office or warehouse or any workplace space planning arrangement .

However, every organization will need a facility manager or manage whose team effectively . When a facility manager begins to apply FM techniques to solve business problems. The case for FM is made. It is a simple matter of demonstrating a qualified return on the investment required. Every organization's success, FM operation of three key activities: they include: needing a proper understanding of the organization's needs, wants, drivers and goals and knowing when needs to review its changing circumstances, developing an effective facilities solution o support the organization's needs, wants , property drives and contribute to achieve its goals both short term and long term, achievement of reliable delivery of that solution in a managed, measured manner.

So, it bring one question: What are the influential factors to be followed the right direction to FM manager's strategic FM operational decision? The influencing factors may include: ownership, governance sector, complexity and perhaps of most significant, the size of the organization's property portfolio.

In fact, major occupiers feel FM service need, they are large corporate organizations and public service organizations. Their aims usually are to raise. The most marginal improvement in efficiency or effectiveness, these aims are the great significance. Major property occupiers will already have a facilities department or individuals performing the FM function with another department like property, finance or human resource, sale and marketing's facilities.

Usually these FM need occupiers who will encounter this problem: How can apply FM service systems and processes to be developed to improve reliable service delivery making use of the economies of scale, not suffering because of the size of the problem. This question will be facility manager individual concerning question: How to apply (FM) technique to solve the improvement reliable service delivery making use of the economics of scale problem for whose organization?

In reality much of external facilities management benefits to organizations, instead of raising efficiency, improving performance, raising productivity, reducing maintenance expenditure, e.g. energy saving, reducing natural resource waste, increasing local employment, improving supply chain management are all elements of the FM contribution to every organization's need. Hence are the work life balance argument and provision of an effective and safe working environment that supports why some organizations feel need (FM) service to support their organizational development.

Moreover, on cost benefit of space saving efficient view point, space service cost reduction is a key driver for all organizations and the medium, or large sized players will benefit directly from a well coordinated facilities strategy. For example, application FM technique to help warehouse or office space area to save 50% space vacancy to let employees can move easily or putting enough furniture or equipment or many stocks can be putted in warehouses . So, paying more rent expenditure to rent or purchasing another new warehouse or office to satisfy workers or employees' working environment to be better need. If the organization has effective (FM) technique, then it has enough space vacancy to supply to the increase stocks number to be putted inside in warehouse and it can let workers to move safety in available to let staffs to move easily and equipment have enough space to be stored in the limited warehouse space problem.

For greater space savings benefits will bring either long term renting or buying of increasing offices or warehouse number expenditure problem to any organizations, when the organizations' cost or renting or buying accommodation probably accounting for 60 to 70% of total occupancy cost . So a strategic program to release space or the prevent the acquisition of moves can be the most significant consideration to any facility manager, with between 40% and 60% of the workplaces are unoccupied in most offices or warehouses at any given moment in time.

Hence, how to apply (FM) technique to save space occupied areas for employment moving or stocks or equipment saving need in offices or warehouses. This issue will be any facility managers' seeking methods to solve problem. However, the important major advantage of facility management to organizations is that the application of management principle to keep the organization's property assets with the aim of maximizing their potentials. Thus, any organizations' facilities have become important, due to the property facilities' worth will increase if the organization's facility management technique can protect the organization's facilities have good performance. Then, the organization's maintenance expenditure will reduce and it won't need to spend expenditure to buy any new facilities to replace old facilities , due to they often damage factor when they are used old.

In conclusion, it explains why effective FM combines resources and activities can raise work environment improvement, which is essential to the raising employee performance aim. For hotel living service case example, this industry must need have good facility management service because hotels must need to fully equipped in term and facilities for effectiveness to satisfy hotel living clients' demand , hotels ought need good facilities asset management style lead to effectiveness in service delivery, there are benefit derivable from the adoption of facilities management from which other hotels can learn from for their effective operations. Hence, it explains why effective FM can bring benefits to hotels' properties to be more comfortable, beautiful appearances to attract many hotel customers to choose to live the hotel. Because hotel's building industrial kitchens, rooms facilities, equipment , halls of categories, restaurant facilities, gum sport entertainment centers' facilities, fans, elevators, lifts, electrical installation, escalators, baking equipment, recreational facilities, including golf courses which will be important factors to influence hotel clients' comfortable living feeling, if the hotel can keep its all facilities in the best living environment often. Then, it can raise chance to attract many hotel customers to choose it to live. So , hotel industry has absolute need to implement effective FM strategy to keep its properties more attractive to satisfy its clients' living needs.

Instead of hotel industry, logistic transportation industry also needs effective facilities management in warehouse, because of the logistic company's warehouse 's facilities are good, then it will assist to raise employee individual efficiency in the safe and system shelve stored facilities in workplace environment and improving performance.

Consequently, it will bring the shorten time to deliver any products to clients to avoide the delaying time delivery in order to let customers to feel more satisfactory to their services. In simple, it seems that some industries need have effective facilities management techniques to help them to bring long term customer satisfactory feeling, worker individual efficiency raising and performance improvement benefits. Hence, it seems facility management techniques' demand will be increased to some industries in popular in the future because it has help to raise employee individual efficiency , productive performance and client individual satisfactory level consequently.

What benefit will bring to the airport if it implement FM strategy?

How important is airport facility management? Without a doubt, facility management is crucial to ensure operational functions around the airport works efficiently. Airports wish to maintain a positive brand image and keep their customers happy with:

consistent services standard to the customer

a smooth airport operation flow

safe and secure environment

a smooth security screening flow

As the airports dealing with the growing capacity on a daily basis, outsourcing facility management services is a great option because it eases the headaches of managing the physical airport. Moreover, airports save costs, enhance the passenger experience, and spend their time to focus on business growth.

Passengers Expectation

Passenger's satisfaction depends on their experience from the minute they reach the airport, expecting to feel relaxed throughout the check-in, waiting and boarding process. The basic requirements for better customer experience at the airport weigh from the speed of baggage delivery, smooth check-in at the airport terminals, little time taken for security checks and the cleanliness of the facilities.

Even though these days most passengers have obtained a boarding pass before they arrive at the airport, however, not knowing how long it will really take to move through the terminal, passengers tend to arrive very early for flights thus spend more time waiting at the airport. The ground experience before passenger boards an aircraft can be divided into these segments:

getting to the airport

waiting in the terminal before security

passing through security checkpoints

finding the gate

Practical check-in facilities improve arrival and departure flow at the airport. Delays for passengers, airport staff and airline crew resulting in disruptions to airport and airline operations. Therefore, airports and airlines will be backed by the airport assistance roles such as:

ground and luggage handling

luggage claim, recovery, sorting and transfer

delivery and placement in plane

cargo and luggage loading and unloading

luggage transfer

runway support

passenger check-in

reception, embarking and disembarking passengers

management of passenger transfers

flight preparation and management

ticketing, excess luggage management

luggage claim, management of irregularities

Beside improvement the flow of departure and arrival at the airport, passengers consider cleanliness to be a valid circumstance (Batra, 2014). As cleanliness can impact customers' first impression of the service (Harris & Sachau, 2005) and experience (Pijls & Groen, 2012), the sanitary condition of a place such as an airport is a fundamental factor. Hence, airports require regular cleaning and maintenance to maintain their image.

An experienced and knowledgeable facility manager for airport assistant and cleaning tasks often result in better quality output which technical and maintenance tasks can be completed faster and more proficiently. Thus, outsourcing airport assistance and cleaning service are the best solutions to meet the passengers' expectation of the airport facilities at any time. Improvement airport operational efficiency

Any major airport has lots of customers which most of them are passengers and airlines crew. The passengers demanded useful facilities to use when check-in, waiting and boarding. Airlines required space for aeroplanes, facilities for routine maintenance, places for passengers and flight crews while on the ground. Air-freight companies needed space for cargo aeroplanes. Pilots and the cabin crew needed runways, facilities for aircraft storage and maintenance, and places to relax while on the ground.

The growing capacity of the airport required good planning and operational efficiency. On-time performance is a major parameter for evaluating operational efficiency of airlines; is directly associated with customer satisfaction, and is positively correlated with profitability (Dresner and Xu, 1995; Steven et al., 2012; Mellat-Parast et al., 2015) Top operational efficiency occurs when the right combination of people, processes, and technology come together to optimize business performance.

So, if the airport can provide a clean and safe workplace , it will increase airport staff productivity. Automating daily operations and administrative tasks are crucial to support the airport staff in providing good services consistently. According to a report commissioned by Amadeus Airport, airports can improve operational efficiency through the digital transformation of processes, well-executed data analytics and insight sharing. While delivering excellent passenger experience and improve its operational efficiency, airports also need to increase non-aeronautical (retail) revenue.

For airports, ensuring passengers enjoy a smooth transit through the airport is vital: Spend increases by 2.5% for every minute a customer is in a retail area and not stuck in a queue (Boston Consulting Group, 2018). According to research done by J.D. Power and Associates (2010), it shows that the happier the passengers were at the airport, the more money they spent in the terminal.

Oursourcing FM to airport organizational benefit

Outsourcing facility management will help you attract and retain happy customer and staff. Through highly visible airport improvements and smooth-running terminal operations, outsourced facility management can deliver long-term cost savings by addressing deferred maintenance energy consumption and sustainability. Airports also get strategic direction and help to oversee day-to-day management works in operations, maintenance, technical and systems integration, infrastructure, retail business and space

management from the outsourced facility management experts.
Safety and Security

Unfortunately, airports are targets for terrorist activity. For that reason, it's vitally crucial that airports take extremely strict security measures. The facility manager guarantees the airport stays safe and secure by monitoring, checking and improving the security systems, video surveillance system and other airport equipment constantly. Failure to do so may lead to undesirable conditions leading to poor operation, loss, injury, prosecution, and insurance claims to the airports.

However, airports are also introducing effective procedures to optimize the workflow during the security screening in the light of the snail-pace queues. By outsourcing technical maintenance and security service, you are granted access to innovative ideas and leading practices from them that will enhance the quality of your facilities and the airport experience overall. They offer new innovation and effective solution that improves the passenger experience, saves costs, creates efficiencies and adds value.
Why does FM is provided to airport , it can provide facility innovation benefit to let travel passengers feel more comfortable to wait in the country 's airport?

To ensure the efficiency and effectiveness of facility management in coordinating demand and supply of airport facilities and services, continuous innovation and new technology development is useful and necessary to achieve high-quality service offering. According to Skytrax's research, being a global travel leader means constantly striving to improve, innovate and impress. A poll conducted by SITA finds airline passengers are happier when technology ease their way through the airports (SITA Passenger IT Insights, 2019).

According to ACI World Director General, Angela Gittens in the Connected Aviation Today that investing in new and improved infrastructure, as well as making the most of existing infrastructure, is the bedrock on which smooth airport operations and improved passenger experiences are built (Seawright, S, 2019). New technology in surveillance monitoring system enabling digital surveillance streams to travel over the internet so that operators in various airport departments such as police, customs, fire and medic, baggage, and airport operations, can all monitor the video feeds from separate PC workstations.

Airports and airlines can take note that technology solutions can boost passenger satisfaction, every step of the way including the cleanliness of their washrooms. The technology-driven initiative, known as ATALIAN Restroom Management System (AMS), is capable of sending an immediate alert to the cleaning staff for swift action if required. We understand how tough it can be for a major airport to run and maintain a smooth operation while working on multi-tasks at the same time.

What is airport Facility Management?

The facility manager guarantees the airport stays safe and secure by monitoring, checking and improving the security systems, video surveillance system and other airport equipment constantly.

What is the role of facility management?

Facilities managers are responsible for the security, maintenance and services of work facilities to ensure that they meet the needs of the organisation and its employees. Facilities managers essentially look after all of the services that helps a business or other organisation do its work.

What are the 3 main tasks of facilities management?

Four Main Functions of FM

Supporting people.

Establishing processes.

Facilities upkeep and improvement.

Technology integration.

Putting it all together for facilities management.

What is the importance of facility in airport?

Practical check-in facilities improve arrival and departure flow at the airport. Delays for passengers, airport staff and airline crew resulting in disruptions to airport and airline operations. Therefore, airports and airlines will be backed by the airport assistance roles such as: ground and luggage handling.

What are the facilities functions of an airport for it to be considered as international?

International airports include customs and international terminal. Passengers can fly abroad through direct or connecting flights. The international airport can also be used for domestic flights apart from the international.

What are the six main functions of a facility?

Understanding the functions of facilities management

Maintaining & optimising facilities.
Streamlining processes.
Supporting people.
Managing projects.
Integrating technology.
Top Five Benefits of Facilities Management
Asset tracking and management. Tracking assets and budgets through spreadsheets is about as convoluted as it gets. ...
Space optimization. ...
System of record. ...
Cost analysis. ...
Integration. ...
Culminating in a better workplace.
What are examples of facility services?
Some examples include:
Heating, cooling, and ventilation (HVAC)
Plumbing and plumbing fixtures.
Lighting and electrical systems.
Mechanical systems outside of HVAC.
Emergency control systems, such as sprinklers.
What are the types of airport facilities?
Facilities
Check-in facilities, including a baggage drop-off.
Security clearance gates.
Passport control (for some international flights)
Gates.
Waiting areas.
Which kind of facilities is required at airport?
OTHER FACILITIES
Pre-paid Taxi Car Service.
Medical Room.
Baby care room.
Money Exchange Services.
Free Passenger baggage trolleys.
Baggage wrapping services.
Parking space for approx.
What are the facilities provided in airport building?
Main Function of Terminal Airport — Change of Movement Type-From car,

train or bus to plane. — Processing (passenger processing space)-Ticket, check-in, security check. — Provide Passenger Facilities - Shopping, toilets, eating, meeting & greeting, business & conference.

What are the airport operations?

Passenger operations include baggage handling and tagging. Terminal operations comprise resource allocation and staff management. Airside operations include aircraft landing and navigation, airport traffic management, runway management, and ground handling safety

How are airports organized?

Airports typically own all of their facilities and make money by leasing them to airlines, air-freight companies, and retail shops and services, as well as by charging for services like fuel and parking and through fees and taxes on airline tickets. The revenues pay off the municipal debt and cover the operating costs.

What is airport Layout?

An Airport Layout Plan (ALP) is a scaled, graphical presentation of the existing and future airport facilities, their location on the airport campus, and pertinent clearance and dimensional information.

What are the challenges of facilities management?

6 facilities management challenges companies face this year

Managing a safe return to the office. ...

Optimizing space utilization in the hybrid workplace. ...

Planning office moves and consolidations. ...

Managing workplace technology. ...

Managing facility maintenance. ...

Rethinking the employee experience.

What is poor facility management?

Buildings are subject to wear and tear or structural depreciation in response to their maintenance neglect which are often manifested in poor facility management. Depreciation in its severe state will reduce the economic lives of buildings and render such buildings in to dilapidation or state of derelict.

What is the critical part of an airport?

In aviation, a critical area refers to a designated area of an airport that all aircraft, vehicles, persons or physical obstructions must remain clear of when one or more Instrument Landing Systems (ILS) are in use, to protect against signal interference or attenuation that may lead to navigation errors, or accident.

What is the need of airport infrastructure?

Role of Airport Infrastructure in National Economy

The quality of airport infrastructure, which is a vital component of the overall transportation network, contributes directly to a country's international competitiveness and the flow of foreign investment.

Why is an airport called an airport?

An airfield would only imply landing strips. An aerodrome added a suffix that implied modernity and more complete facilities, even paved runways, and an airport offered complete facilities for aggregating, moving or receiving, and disaggregating large volumes of people and cargo.'

What are the four airport components?

Components of Airport may include:

Runway.

Taxiway.

Apron.

Terminal building.

Control tower.

Hanger.

Parking.

What is terminal facility?

As used in these regulations the term terminal facilities means all facilities, including waiting room, rest room, eating, drinking, and ticket sales facilities which a motor carrier makes available to passengers of a motor vehicle operated in interstate or foreign commerce as a regular part of their transportation.

What are the 3 key functions undertaken by airports?

Direct effects. Include the activities undertaken at the airport itself: services to passengers (check-in, security, boarding), cargo (loading and unloading), and aircraft (refueling, cleaning).

What are the three parts of an airport?

It includes runways, taxiways, and ramps.

Runway – An area where aircraft takes off and lands. It is made of soft grass, asphalt, or concrete. ...

Ramp – Also called Apron, this area is used for parking the aircrafts. ...

Taxiway – It is a path on the airport that connects the ramp to the runway.

What are the functional areas of an airport?

Departments of Airport

Airport Services English text.

Medical Center.

Postal freight services.

Air Security Service (Security group, control and inspection group)

Department of Accounting and Reporting.

Service for Electrical and technical illumination for the fights.

What is airport Master Plan?

An Airport Master Plan is a critical planning tool for determining the future requirements of an airport and provides a vision for realizing its ultimate potential.

What are the three sections of an airport?

It is customary to classify the several components of an airport in three major catego- ries: airside facilities; landside facilities; and the terminal building, which serves as the interchange between the management alliances: Problems of competition and complexity

Airport facilities management alliances: Problems of competition and complexity

Airport facilities management (AFM) is being delivered through collaboration with airports, through forming networks and strategic alliances. Facilities management (FM) is a function that is adapting because of a changing external environment; strategic alliances is one method used by FM to deliver this change in strategy. This article explores and examines the structure and characteristics of AFM alliances including the problems faced by competition and managerial complexity. This article explores the AFM function, its importance to airports and its strategic and competitive direction. The article concludes that although there are inherent problems in AFM arrangements, these can be effectively managed through well-written contractual documentation.

FM can be defined broadly as a function that consists of numerous managerial activities. More recently, FM is considered to be an integrated approach to operating, maintaining, improving and adapting the buildings and infrastructure of an organisation, to ensure that the built environment supports the primary objectives of the host organisation (Nutt, 2004). In airports, the management activities could be grouped into five main areas: information management, building and property management, civil services, procurement and logistics management, and legal services. FM functions focus on planning and act as a coordinating unit within the firm, aiming to ensure that the function acts as the driving force behind successful operations (van Wagenberg, 1997). The ability of the FM function to translate organisational and individual needs into a balanced and flexible supply of supporting service within an environment that supports these needs is considered one of the successful functions of FM (Klee, 1997).

Increasingly, the primary objectives of organisations are required, or strongly urged, to include environmental commitments. In order for FM to continue to set an environment where the client organisation can deliver its core and supporting business functions, it is likely that FM will need to adapt its processes to include energy management and sustainably orientated processes. This will involve change at the strategic level and would involve the combination of many resources and personnel to design, and redesign the facilities to suit the end user and the system in which the building is used (Edum-Fotwe, 2001; Nutt, 2004). Alternatively, it can be viewed that because there is significant evidence to suggest that the risk of climate change is significant, it should be addressed by all FM managers (Warren, 2010); climate change could legitimately be viewed as a business continuity issue, with natural disasters posing as a risk to the continuation of service provision to a building. Facilities managers have a key role to play in the development of an organisation's Building Continuity Management plan (Warren, 2010). Longer term security of energy supply is an increasingly important issue (Warren, 2010). This is another issue that will require the involvement, if not the total management by, from FM with their knowledge and management of the building systems. The European focus on CO_2 emission reductions and resultant government reduction targets for the built environment are aiming at reducing energy use by encouraging the more efficient use and adaptation of building systems and technology (Williams, 2008). Again FM can have a significant impact on the introduction of sustainable building operations. Strategic alliances have been found to be effective where technological change is the aim (Rothaermel, 2000), adding strength to the notion of using strategic alliances to develop sustainable FM.

The methods to deliver the developing FM function can be described under separate business models: integrated business unit, empowered business unit ('selling' its services to the company), an internal profit-centre or an independent FM service provider (third-party provider). These business models, respectively, can be seen as a life cycle process. The higher the strategic importance of the FM function to the company, the more likely the FM function will be performed by either an internal profit-centre or by an independent provider (Gaya Walters, 1997; Ytsma, 1997). When the

FM function is performed by a profit-centre, the FM organisation will try to sell its services outside the company. The most important aspects of the profit-centre are the commercialisation and the performance responsibility of the FM function. When the acquisition of FM services takes place from an independent provider, a higher degree of control is required; this results in a shift from functional FM towards relationship management and the management of cooperative agreements (Gaya Walters, 1997).

Many airports split up their AFM functions into technical, infrastructure, commercial and space management (Frankfurt AFM, 2003; Munich AFM, 2003). Technical management consists of maintaining and developing all technical systems needed to operate an airport. This wide service ranges from vehicle maintenance, security and fire protection down to small technical services. The infrastructure management involves logistics management, including parking, public transport and also the arrangement of cleaning staff, medical services and workplace development. The commercial management function mainly controls relations with third parties (for example, retailers) and contractors, but also performs functions such as business administration and marketing. Airport space management includes building, property and surface management. It provides a framework to support all the other AFM activities.

On conclusion, any airport organizations ought need to implement FM strategy in order to provide comfortable and service performance improvement feeling to encourage any countries travel passengers choose to go to the country to travel or change airplanes in order to raise airport income during any airline air planes renting staying number increases and travel passsnger shopping number increases in the country's airport .

reference

Aaltola, M. (2005) The international airport: The hub-and-spoke pedagogy of the American empire. Global Networks 5 (3): 261–278.

Adler, N. and Berechman, J. (2001) Evaluating multi-hub networks in a deregulated aviation market with an application to Western Europe. Transportation Research, Part A 35: 373–390.

Advani, A. (1999) Passenger-friendly airports: Another reason for airport privatization. Policy Study, Report No. 254. The Reason Public Policy Institute: Los Angeles, pp. 1–26.

Bhadra, D. and Hechtman, D. (2004) Determinants of airport hubbing in the United States: An empirical framework. Public Works Management and

Policy 9: 26–50.

Brown, A.W. and Pitt, M.R. (2001) Measuring the facilities management influence in delivering sustainable airport development and expansion. Facilities 19 (5/6): 222–232.

Cranfield University. (2002) Study on the Competition between Airports and the Application of State aid Rules. Final report. Vol. 1, European Commission, DG Energy and Transport, Directorate F-Air Transport.

Edum-Fotwe, F.T. (2001) Review: Facility management: Risks & opportunities. In: B. Nutt and P. McLennan (eds.) Oxford, UK: Blackwell Science, 2000. ARCOM Newsletter, 2, 6–7.

Freathy, P. and O'Connel, F. (1999) Planning for profit: Commercialization of European airports. Long Range Planning 32 (6): 587–597.

Gaya Walters, B. (1997) Organisatiemodellen. In: W. Ytsma (ed.) De vele gezichten van facilities management. Deventer, the Netherlands: Kluwer Bedrijfsinformatie.

Kesharwani, T. (2000) Rapidly growing private presence in airports takes several different forms. ICAO Journal 55 (3): 8–9.

Killing, J.P. (1988) Understanding alliances: The role of task and organizational complexity. In: F.J. Contractor and P. Lorange (eds.) Cooperative Strategies in International Business: Joint Ventures and Technology Partnerships between Firms. Massachusetts/Toronto: Lexington Books.

Klee, H. (1997) Facilities management: een terreinafbakening. In: W. Ytsma (ed.) De vele gezichten van facilities management. Deventer, the Netherlands: Kluwer Bedrijfsinformatie.

Lorange, P. and Roos, J. (1992) Strategic Alliances: Formation, Implementation and Evolution. Cambridge, UK: Wiley-Blackwell.

Nutt, B. (2004) Infrastructure and facilities: Forging alignments between supply and demand. Conference Proceeding of Future in Property and Facility Management II, A Two-day International Conference, University College London, London.

Park, S.H. and Ungson, G.R. (2001) Interfirm rivalry and managerial complexity: A conceptual framework of alliance failure. Organization Science 12 (1): 37–53.

Pels, E., Nijkamp, P. and Rietveld, P. (2003) Inefficiencies and scale economics of European airport operations. Transportation Research Part E: Logistics and Transportation Review 39 (5): 341–361.

Percoco, M. (2010) Airport activity and local development: Evidence from Italy. Urban Studies 47 (11): 2427–2443.

Pitt, M.R. (2001) Strategic direction in the airport business: Enabling or disabling? Facilities 19 (3/4): 150–156.

Pitt, M.R. and Brown, A.W. (2001) Developing a strategic direction for airports to enable the provision of both network and low-fare carriers. Facilities 19 (1/2): 52–60.

Pitt, M.R., Wai, F.K. and Teck, P.C. (2001) Strategic optimization of airport passenger buildings. Facilities 19 (11/12): 413–418.

Rothaermel, F.T. (2000) Technological discontinuities and the nature of competition. Technology Analysis & Strategic Management 12 (2): 149–160.

Schiphol Airport Annual Report (2002) Schiphol Group. http://www.schiphol.nl/SchipholGroup/InvestorRelations/ FinancialInformation/AnnualReports.htm.

Tay, L. (2006) Strategic facilities management of Suntec Singapore International Convention and Exhibition Centre. Facilities 24 (3/4): 120–131.

CHAPTER TWO

AIRLINE AND AIRPORT TRANSPORT STRATEGY

In airline transport industry strategy, I shall attempt to indicate some useful strategies to help airlines to keep travellers number in order to avoid to reduce. I shall indiate as below:

● Airline Oil Price Variable Factor strategy

1.1 Positive social change influence to vehicle fuel consumers

What suitation is positive social change to vehicle fuel consumers. We are entering globalizational competitive society, such as airline fuel case, if the country, e.g. US is increasing vehicle consumers in this year, then US vehicle fuel demand will increase. So, the US vehicle fuel price will be caused to increase. Due to much vehicle fuel demand increases in US this year, so foreign fuel import and US fuel manufacturers will increase to supply to US for vehicle market in this year, due to many US vehicle consumers need to buy fuel to drive their vehicles in US. However, due to fuel natural resource will have limited number to be supplied to manufacture airline fuel, due to much fuel is used to manufacture vehicle fuel in US this year. So, it will cause airline fuel manufacturing and supply shortage challenge. Due to this year, US decreases airline fuel supply, but the US airlines demands fuel number is still increasing. Consequently, vehicle fuel increasing demand factor will cause airline fuel price to be rised in US this year.

For example, air tickets can be bought from internet, so travellers won't need to go to travel agent to buy conventienty. It is due to the global travel industry is increasingly competition. Thus, global travel industry competition will bring negative social change to influences fuel price rising because it will increase traveller numbers and airline flight times to fly. When, traveller's travelling desire demand numbers will be grown up fastly, then their online electronic-ticket buying or consumption behaviors will be rise. Thus, it will also cause online e-ticket price is decreased to attract many travellers to choose to buy e-ticket from online channel more than paper-ticket visiting travel agent channel. Thus, it is negative social change influences to cause fuel price rising due to plane flight flying times will increase and airline company will increase demand to buy many fuel to prepare to fly often. When fuel demand will rise, then the fuel sellers will rise fuel price in possible. Thus, airline industry global competition will being negative social change to influence fuel price raising up and air ticket price falling down to attract many traveller numbers to choose to buy among different travel agents.

Negative social change influence

What suitation is positive social change. I shall indicate economic growth example. When one country has better economic development in the year. Then, employers will have more effort to do businesses. Then, they will create many jobs to provide to the country citizen to do. When, these unemployed people have jobs to do, they will have extra income to save. They can spend extra to prepare to spend to enjoy their entertainment every year, such as travelling. Thus, the positive social change will influence traveller number increasing, then the plane fliging flying times will also increase, it will cause planes need to use much fuel to fly. The result, it will also increase fuel demand, but the fuel natural resource number will decrease , so fuel supply will also decrease. Finally, it will also cause fuel price to be risen.

Also, I shall indicate the financial risk of airline industry evidence from Cathay Pacific airways and China airlines against key determinants of which include interest rate, exchange rate and fuel price risk for the period of January 1996 year to December 2011 year. During this period, these key external factors which were the most serious influence to cause these two airlines choose to change their strategic behaviors.

Due to any these financial risks is difficult to predict and it was also changing often, these factors will also affect any airlines stock returns which arise from changing economic conditions, e.g. fuel price movements and fluctuations in exchange rates. These external unpredicted changing factors will attribute to the air tickets cyclical demand, capital investment, fixed costs of labor and landing rights to this global airline industry.

However, the relationship between fuel price and stock prices varies across economies. The effects of oil price changes in sub-sector indices, such as wood, paper and printing, insurance and electricity. In the past, on global stock exchange market was positively significant in 2011 year. Otherwise, with respect to the U.S.A. aviation industry, some economists suggested that global airlines stock returns were negatively to percentage change in fuel prices related to any airline firm value, e.g. Qantas and Air New Zealand were negatively share price growth to fuel price risk in the short term in the 2011 year.

Thus, it brings this question. Whether positive or negative social change will be one important factor to impact fuel price rising. I feel positive social or negative social change will be one important factor to impact fuel price rising. The reason is such as below:

Nowadays, airline transportation demands are increasing, due to many travelers need to catch planes to travel as well as many cargoes need to be carried to planes to transport to different countries to sell. It seems aviation transportation industry is important to influence the health of the global economy growth nowadays. However, ignorance of internal or external market dynamics, catching travelers business can be detrimental to airline profitability more than carrying cargoes business. Because the demands of travelling different countries' travelers' consumption are still more than the demands of businessmen carrying cargoes in any countries every year. Thus, the travel industry will increase demand to human travelling business more than cargo transportation business. However, the cargo flying transporation demand will rise, due to many global fast speed post businesses are growing. Base on both global cargo flying transportation demand and travellers' flying travelling demand are increasing. Thus, the fuel demand will increase, but the fuel supply will be shortage. So, it will cause fuel price rising consequently.

How can positive or negative social change influence any airlines' air ticket prices to be risen or fallen? In fact, the increase in petroleum price can have chance to affect airlines in a negative manner because increased oil prices have resulted in the reduction of services operations, the number of airline schedules flights, even airline bankruptcies.

Thus, it seems that plan travellers and air flying cargo transportation both demand have been increasing. This social increasing demand change factor, it will be the most influential cause the bad effects to cause airline industry share price reducing or reducing air ticket price or decreasing traveler numbers more than the other factors influence, such as inflation, terrorism, oil shortage, bank interest rate etc. unpredictable external suitation factors. To support this hypotheses, this are my research questions, such as : Does a combination of terrorism and price of petroleum significantly influence airline profit changing mostly? The alternative hypothesis was base on a significant relationship exists between terrorism, price of petroleum and airline profitability more than other factors, such as inflation, bank interest rate or air ticket price changing of these factors influence. I shall indicate that the first assumption was that terrorism has a negative effect on airline profitability and another assumption was that only external factors as oil prices or terrorism affect airline profitability.

Terrorisms attack influence

Whether terrorisms attack will influence fuel price rises up or falls down. I feel terrorisms attack to any country, which will cause plan fuel price falls down. Because travellers will feel dangerous and worry about their life safety when they catch the plan to enter the country if the country has serious terrorisms attack risk to cause plan crash accidently.

However the effects of oil price and terrorism on airline profitability was limited to a regional perspective, e.g. the terrorism attack of plane crash event to USA on 11 Sept. After the terrorism attack happened on USA 11 Sept. incident of terrorism attack was restricted to events of skyjacking, attacks on oil production, refinery and distribution. Thus, USA on 11 Sept. terrorism attack will cause oil price falls down , due to it will influence travellers fear death , so who will reduce times to travel to USA after 11 Sept. date terrorism attack occurrence at the year. The oil sellers will reduce oil sale price to attract many airline companies to buy more supply, due to airlines will decrease demand to buy fuel to provide planes to fly when the traveller numbers has decreasing and flying times will be decrease also. Thus, the fuel price will be decreased consequently after the terrorism attacks to any country.

Other types of terrorist activities, such as attacks on financial targets or senior government officials could have an adverse effect on the petroleum and airline industry. I think the disruption of the production or distribution of petroleum because of incidents of terrorism was costly in terms of loss of business and the inflationary effect on fuel dependent products or services.

In fact, some airlines have adopted more fuel saving technology, so whose fuel consumption would not use more than other non fuel saving technology airlines. So, the owned fuel saving technology airlines which will buy less fuel to use. It means that they won't need fear fuel rising to increase their expenditure because they only need to buy less fuel to use and their fuel demand won't fall , even fuel price has risen.

However, it seems fuel price increasing will not be the only factor to influence the airline industry's traveler numbers decreasing, due it is possible that the airlines need to rise air ticket price to riase their profit, sue to their fuel cost has risen. However, due to some airlines which have fuel saving technology, so which can avoid to use more fuel to provide planes to use and which fuel costs will be reduced, then which can provide cheaper air ticket fare prices to compare the non fuel saving technology airlines. The result will cause some non owned fuel save technological airlines will lose travelling customers in this global airline travelling market, also the non fuel saving technology airlines need to renew their fuel technology if which want to keep their competitive abilities to avoid to close down their businesses.

Can airline fuel self-organization avoid
fuel price rising cost

I feel one airline fuel self-organization can avoid fuel price rising to influence cost rising because it doesn't often buy any fuel from fuel suppliers. However, there are some airlines which are the characteristic of airline fuel self organization and they are present in that both of oil fuel production and providing flights service in airline industry. So, these airline fuel self organizations can control the oil fuel price by themselves. However, one airline fuel self organization is also evident in efforts by businesses acts of terrorism against economic targets by adopting proactive steps, such as airline and airport security. So, it seems airline fuel self organization can reduce the risk to avoid oil price raising and terrorism attacks to raise cost in airline industry risk management sector.

Beside, these airline fuel self organizations which have high technology of fuel efficient aircrafts, the use of one aircraft model, the adoption of direct routes versus customer loyalty programs and other operational cost reductions are strategies for increased profitability. It seems these airline fuel self organizations can solve oil price, terrorism etc. external factor influences to raise cost.

Instead of high technology of fuel efficient aircrafts and airline fuel self organization methods can solve terrorism attacks and oil price rising risks. However, I believe that there are other risks are caused to these airline fuel self organizations to raise their airline cost possibly. The risks include such as user factor, such as culture, tradition, education ; economic factor, such as costs, human resources and macro economic factor, such as political stability, economic development, educational policy, health policy, environmental policy. However, these risks occurrences are resulting in the relationship of cause and effect events. These events are not directly observable. Such as, the complexity of relationship between terrorism and airline profitability. Hence, if global airline industry can predict when those risks occur to do protective strategic behavior. It is possible that which can understand when these risk events will occur and to adopt their protective strategic behaviors to influence their outcomes to be positive to avoid any external risk threats on the long term. However, I think hierarchy, airlines fuel self organization efficiency methods which are as possible predictors of user preferences to avoid risk threat events to cause whose airline businesses cost rising to cause failure occurrences in airline industry.

Can tourism industry influence airline profitability

In my study, I suppose terrorism and the price of petroleum both factors which had properties of distinct and interrelated close relationship to raise airline cost. Moreover, these variables (terrorism and the price of petroleum) displayed differentiation, self replication, efficiency and hierarchy which can cause risk events to airline industry. However, I also think the other internal and external threat factors of airline industry, such as inflation, bank interest rate, business model, service quality, airline fuel or plane engine technology, air ticket pricing, brand loyalty, airline strategic management, government policy and fuel hedging of these factors which can also raise the risks to threaten any airlines existence in airline industry. There are two basic business models in tourism industry. They are network (full service) and low cost (discount) carriers. The network carrier model employs diversification strategy by increased domestic destinations, serving international routes, providing diverse seating arrangements (business, economy and first class), maintaining a complex system of offering high quality service. Otherwise, low cost (discount) airlines focus on lower air fares. To keep operating costs down, discount airlines offer shorter routes and provide point-to-point destinations rather than through sophisticated flights are primarily in domestic destinations. So, discount airlines operate a common model aircraft fleet, offer a single seating arrangement and cheaper flight services offered to compare network airlines. However, these two basic business models have their unique competitive abilities to provide any airlines existence in tourism industry nowadays.

In fact, natural resource of oil is decreasing in our earth. But as the same time, human demand is increasing and oil supply is decreasing, so it also causes the oil fuel price is increasing to supply to airline industry. It influences not only to airline industry, it also impacts of higher oil fuel price to tourism, such as expansion of airports are made based on expected demand increase.

Tourism has been proven to many adverse events, including terrorism, flight disruptions. Beside, the bad natural climate change influences, such as the volcanic ash cloud event occurred in April 2010 year. So, airline industry need to concern climate change because it will cause high fuel prices indirectly. For example, the event occurred the extreme increase in operating costs for airlines in 2008 year, due to unprecedented prices for aviation fuel also meant, that despite the introduction of fuel charges, so this event causes the global tourism industry recorded losses seriously. Even if alternative fuels become commercially available for airlines which are still likely to be more expensive than present aviation fuel.

Higher airfares in the future are likely to lead to reduction in travel and cause tourists to shift from more distant to closer destination. When some of the economic responses to higher oil prices are obvious assessing the overall economic impacts on tourism is difficult. However, long term changes in global oil price rises will be similar to global changes in other commodity prices, exchange rates and income. It is therefore important to consider the impact of high oil prices on tourism from a general equilibrium perspective rather than relying only on bottom partial equilibrium approaches.

However, I believe tourism and airline industries have close relationship, such as tourism and airline industries are likely to suffer in an environment of high oil prices. Given that tourism destinations receive tourists from a range of origins, it would be useful to understand of some countries are increasing oil prices than others. Such as the net oil importing countries are selling higher oil prices than oil exporting countries generally. For example, New Zealand is an oil import country to provide planes for international visitor arrivals, so its oil fuel price is usually higher to charge to NZ airlines because any NZ airlines need to pay to foreign countries to buy any oil more expensive price. So, NZ airlines usually charge higher airfares to its visitors to compare the other exporting oil countries' airlines. It will impact NZ has negative influence to domestic tourism industry as well as planes need will also be decreased , due to NZ charge high fuel price to cause air ticket price to be raised.

In economic theory, on income effects indicate negative impacts on tourism demand, the exact effects of higher oil fuel prices for specific destinations are far from clear. However, airline industry's different market segments show different sensitivities to air ticket fares changes.

On the first hand, if the visitors are long destinations generally wealthier than average and therefore potentially less affected, as energy costs would be a smaller proportion of their income compared will be those from less wealthy groups. Thus, the more wealthier travelers who won't decrease travelling desire, even the fuel price raises to case the air ticket price to be increased.

On the second hand, oil prices don't translate into higher transport costs especially not on air routes that are highly competitive and that are maintained for strategic reasons. So, non air transportation industry won't influence customer number to be decreased easily.

On the third hand, many other factors shape tourists' decision making, including emotion drivers or those related to images, fashions and perceptions. Increasing environmental protection awareness of tourists could also be an important factor to influence tourism consumption, instead of oil fuel price raising causes air ticket fares raising factor to reduce traveler numbers. However, oil price raising reason causes also due to high use of cars, vans and domestic air transport in some countries, e.g. Hong Kong, China countries, there are many people like to buy cars to drive. So, the private driver numbers are increasing demand to cause these countries' oil fuel prices raise in the short time suddenly. It implies airlines need to consider their country car number whether is increasing or decreasing. If their country car number is increasing, it is possible to cause fuel price to be risen up because car demand is increasing to need to use more fuel and it has less supply of fuel in the year. Otherwise, if their country car number is decreasing, it is possible to cause fuel price to be fallen down because car demand is decreasing to need to use less fuel and it has more supply of fuel in the year.

Is fuel price rising only factor to cause airline risk
in short term

In long run, fuel raising price will not cause risk to airline, due to implications of changes to supply and demand side conditions of oil fuel energy may differ qualitatively. For example, due to investment responses of producers, consumers and governments in alternative energy sources and more energy efficient plants, vehicles are supplied in order to achieve oil fuel price can't be risen seriously.

However, I believe oil fuel rising charge will be an important factor to influence global airline ticket fares to be increased in the short term to cause risk because oil fuel rising charge will be influenced to raise any airlines pressure from other unpredicted factor risk influences.

Firstly, on the bank interest changing factor, e.g. bank interest rate rising which only attract more bank saving. But it can not influence the bank savers who choose to reduce relax time to go to other countries travelling. Otherwise, when the bank savers can save more money to earn higher interest in banks, who will prefer to choose to use their saving to consume travelling. Due to who can earn higher interest rate after a period of saving time. So, I believe who behavioral travelling consumption will be raised when the banks will raise interest rate, then the bank savers won't choose to save more money in banks. So it is possible that who will withdraw more money to consume to go to travelling from banks. It seems bank interest rate changing won't influence bank savers' behavioral travelling consumption to be reduced.

Secondly, on the exchange rate changing factor, although any country's exchange changing will cause other countries' money value to be fallen down or risen up. However, it won't influence any travelers' behavioral consumption to be reduced seriously. Although, it is possible that the traveler won't spend too much to go to shopping when who travel to the another country and arrive the country. But, it is not possible to influence the traveler decides to reduce consumption to buy any air ticket to go to travelling in short time.

Thirdly, any country inflation also can not reduce travelers' travelling consumption easily because inflation can influence consumers who choose to buy cheaper foods and clothing and reduce entertainments in their every day life. But, one country's inflation can not influence it's citizen do not spend much travelling expenditure because travelers only spend one time or two times of travelling every year usually. So, the travelling expenditure rate of any households is not too much to compare daily essential expenditure.

So, it seems that bank interest rate and exchange rate changing and inflation won't influence any travelers' travelling consumption of decisions to be reduced easily in short time. Otherwise, if the oil fuel price raises too much, then global airlines' cost will be raised in long term. So, the airlines only choose to increase their air fare prices to aim to avoid loss possibly in long term. It seems that oil fuel raising price and bank interest rate and exchange rate changing and inflation factors will have direct influence airline income in long term.

● Methods to solve rising air fare prices to decrease travellers'demand
Biofuels energy increases supply
I suggest these methods how to avoid the oil raising price factor to cause airline air fare prices to be risen to lead the risk of traveler numbers to be reduced as below:

The first method: Whether aviation fuel markets will have what benefits from biofuels supply to planes. I shall refer the scope includes trends in jet fuel price, airline response to fuel price, increases and volatility and environmental goals for aviation. The aviation fuel supply industry includes production, distribution and consumption of aviation fuel and it outlines players in the aviation fuel supply chain. For example, at each airport, fuel supply chain organization and fuel sourcing could differ with regard to the role of oil companies, airlines, airport owners and operators and airport service companies. However, major jet fuel purchasers are airlines, general aviation operators, corporate aviation and the military, with most of the jet fuel in global different countries demanders being used for domestic commercial and civilian flights carrying passengers, cargos or both.

Commercial aviation fuel efficiency has improved dramatically over time, largely due to aircraft and engine upgrades and operational and air traffic control improvements. So, it seems that fuel supply factor can influence airline fare prices majorly. However, jet fuel prices generally correlate with prices of crude oil and other refined petroleum products, such as diesel. So, increasing prices and the persistent price volatility of jet fuel markets import airline industry finances in any countries.

However, airlines use various strategies to manage aviation fuel price certainty, including financial hedges, increased vertical integration and adjustments in aircraft utilization and size to avoid the jet fuel raising price risk.

Investments in alternative aviation fuel could be a mechanism to diversity expose to the price of petroleum. It seems the use of alternative aviation fuel would serve to diversify the fuel mix to reduce the risk of jet fuel monopoly raising price threat. If a diversified fuel mix were to avoid either fuel raising price in short term or to avoid fuel raising price in long term.

Potential benefits include reduced actual fuel costs from only choice of jet fuel supply increased price certainty and lessened fuel costs. This diversify could allow airlines to become more consistently profitable and to make other investments in their businesses.

So, biofuels have potential to meet aviation industry needs, possibly including managing risks of upward fuel price trends and fuel price volatility and avoid risks with greenhouse gas emissions. So, the aviation fuels market could use biofuels to reduce greenhouse gas emission and mitigate long-term upward price trends, fuel price volatility or both.

What are the challenges of high priced oil for aviation? In fact, nowadays not the resources of oil as such, but much more the insecurity of supply, due to geopolitical instability in combination with a tight oil market makes a scenario with much higher oil prices than the world is currently experiencing not unlikely.

Aviation is completely dependent upon oil as its fuel source. Since no practical energy substitute is readily available for commercial aviation, a scarcity of petroleum relative to demand will present a major aviation policy. In addition, efficiency gains, due to operational measures and new aircraft medium term. In particular, it has been demonstrated that the annual reduction rate in fuel consumption traffic unit is not a constant, but is itself also falling, in contrast to past estimates.

So, a high-priced oil scenario will have severe consequences for demand, airline revenues, the competitive position of airports and eventually airline networks, strategies and fleet development. In particular, transfer demand, short-haul and leisure traffic can be expected to be heavily affected by high oil prices, due to their relative high price sensitivity. Also, different countries' governments or/and airlines are valuable to research another new and potential biofuel energy to substitute oil energy to supply our planes to reduce the threat of oil monopoly supply to influence the cause of air fare raising prices. Because the elasticity is very high to travelers, when the travelers feel air fares are rising high or even low level to influence travelers who will choose not to buy the air tickets to go to travel easily.

Whether will the fuel (oil based inputs) risk be high to compare other costs, e.g. engineering maintenance, employees salaries, general cleaning, security office expenses etc. expenditures to airlines? If the probability-weighted upside effect on firm value when a risk is resolved favorably is greater the risk than the probability-weighted downside effect if the risk is resolved badly, then expected value work not be enhanced by hedging. So, the risk will be resolved badly to any commercial airlines.

Airlines are an interesting case because the direct effect of source of risk resides squarely within the no offset in revenue functions (unlike for oil producers, for example), so value effects from costs feed directly into equity value. Most directly, the risk source is fuel costs to commercial airlines. Jet fuel is of course, a mix product of crude oil, so airlines indirectly face oil price risk. There are reasons to expect that airlines' fuel costs might to convex in oil price (i.e. absent any hedging). For example, oil prices, being generally pro-cyclical in recent times, tend to be highest when airline demand is strong.

In conclusion, airlines are therefore apt to use more high priced fuel than low-priced fuel over time. Airlines can raise air fare benefit is limited by the elasticity of demand. Also, cost functions could be influenced from fuel cost corresponds to upturns in economic activity overall (due to demand pressures on oil related prices), so it causes that airline's capacity delivers their services given their level of fixed capital. The essence of airlines basis risk in the case of jet fuel is essentially the time profile of the refining margin between crude and jet fuel, or the time profile of the price differential between other refined distillates and jet fuel. Thus, it is far from clear that risk management with oil is sure to add value to any airlines. It seems the impact of airline energy and any countries' domestic or foreign airline passenger travel numbers which have direct close relationship.

Reducing terrorism occurrence

Can reduce terrorism occurence to reduce airline failure risk? It needs to judge to determine if a combination of terrorism and the price of petroleum significantly predicted airline profitability and which variable whether the further period was the most significant between the terrorism occurrence and the price of petroleum influence.

I suggest that different countries' governments or airlines need to collect samples of financial records from which country's any airline commercial passengers and cargo airlines on costs of fuel and any airline profitability. Also, gathering the terrorism data were comparison of terrorist attacks on petroleum in oil-producing nations, and incidents of high jacking aboard any country's aircraft.

When any countries' airlines or governments can judge whether the impact of airline energy and terrorism risk level is high or middle or low level. Then, which can use this sample data to measure how to do positive social change to decide either ought rise or reduce employment in commercial aviation industry, or ought need to invest other higher commercial activity in tourist and other travel related service businesses and when is the most right time to adopt of green technologies by the civil aviation manufacturing industry after the terrorism attacks occurrence to any country. It seems that any countries' governments or airlines which ought concern that the event of when the terrorism attacks will occur and gather past sample data to predict when the next time terrorism attacks event will be occurred and the risk will be high or middle or low level to influence global airline industry development.

Will airline industry's ticket price elasticity be influenced by demand and supply factor

In fact, the airline industry is largely dependent on the supply of the oil industry. Otherwise, the oil industry is inelastic. However, the increase or decrease of the price of airfare is directly related to the increase or decrease of the oil's price to fuel the aircrafts because there has no any new energy which can be substituted to oil fuel to airline industry.

So, it seems oil fuel producers are monopolies to control its sale price to be raised easily. Another factor that can affect airline industry to be directly targeted by a tragedy brought about by terrorism. The past four years, from 2001 year to 2005 year, there had been at least $40 billion worth of losses in the airline industry because of the September 11 date terrorism attacks in 2000 year. There had been an expected and significant decrease in the demand for the airline industry services because of the attacks that involved planes hijacking and crashing into key locations like the World Trade Center and the Pentagon in USA. Although, terrorism attacks can bring risk to influence fuel price rising in airline industry. However, this risk occurrence to airline industry is only that after the terrorism attacks occurred. It is possible that terrorism attacks won't occur again in the future.

Otherwise, our concerning ought be the greenhouse emissions and how it affects global warming. The air quality would be better once this new regulations are adopted. However, it would affect large airlines. So, it would increase the price of airfares because of economic fees that airline companies have to cover. Air pollution can give a negative impact on the domestic or oversea owned airline companies for long term. If airlines' planes can use clean fuel to fly, e.g. biofuel, then it will bring benefits to global airlines for long term.

On the positive side, the environment would be healthier as the earth's temperature would rise, and greenhouse effect would be dramatically reduced. This positive effect can come at a cost that is greater than most people perceive. On the psychology view point on travelers, who will be more preferable to catch planes to go to different countries to travel, due to the chance of air pollution and global environmental warm issues will be reduced to low risk to influence our health if planes can use biofuel to be energy to fly in the future one day.

It seems that spending expenditure to research other non polluted biofuel new energy is one solvable method to global airline industry in the future. To solve, any airlines or countries' governments or oil producers ought choose to spend more time to research new biofuel. Otherwise, the predicting when terrorism attacks event will be occurred, it is more difficult to predict the time more than researching to produce new biofuel energy method in the future. So, I recommend that researching the new biofuel energy or other kinds of energy to substitute the oil energy is the urgent behavioral economy which the airlines or oil producers or different countries' governments which need to concern nowadays.

● Boeing 747 manufacturing fuel cost strategy

For Boeing 747 air plane manufacture example, how it can help airline to avoid travellers number reduces. Boeing 747 air plane manufacture company how achieve air plane manufacturing strategy to reponse airline traveller number market changing. What is fuel conservation strategy to Boeing 747 air plane manufacturing firm? The cost index, (CI) feature of the flight manufacturing computer (FMC) can help airlines significantly reduce operating cost. However, many operators do not take full advantages of this powerful tool. What does CI ratio mean? The CI is the ratio of the time-related cost of an air plane opertation and the cost of fuel. The value of the CI reflects the relative effects of the fuel cost on overall trip cost as compares to time-related direct operating costs.

The equation form, CI= time cost-\$/hour / fuel cosst -cents/lb

The numerator of the Ci is often called time refrated direct operating cost (minue the cost of fuel). Items, such as flight crew wages can have an hourly cost associated with them, or they may be a fixed cost and have n variation with flying time engines, anxiliary power units, and air planes can be leased by the hour or owned, and maintenance costs can be accounted for an air planes by the hour, by the calendar or by cycles . As a result, each of these items may have a direct hourly cost or a fixed cost over a calendar period with limited or no correlation to flying time.

What does this air plane fuel, cost strategy advantages to airline companies? In the case of high direct time costs, the airline may direct to time costs, the airline may choose to use a larger CI to minimize time and thus cost . In this case, where most costs are fixed, the CI is potentially very low because the airline is primarily trying to minimize fuel cost. Pilots can easily understand minimizing fuel consumption, but it is more difficult to understand minimizing cost when something other than fuel dominates. So, the cost of the CI ratio. Although, this seems straight toward, issues such among the operating locations, fuel tankering, and fuel hedging can make this calculation complicated. So , this fuel consumption cost, air plan manufacturing strategy can help any airlines to reduce air fuel useful cost and waste fuel.

However, CI can be an extremely useful way to manage operating costs. Because CI is a function of both fuel and non-fuel costs. It is important to use it appropriately to gain the greatest benefit. Appropriate use varies with each airline, and perhaps for each flight.

How low fuel situations can bring less fuel consumed benefit in the more environmentally friendly flight? Fuel conservation strategy can help airlines significantly reduce operating costs. However, many operators do not take full advantage of this powerful tool. Cruise flight is the phase of flight that falls the largest percentages of trip time and trip fuel are consumed typically in this phase of flight, which also impact trip time and fuel significantly can often be avoided through appropriate cruise planning. This fuel conservation strategy includes these characteristics. These objectives which depend on the perspective of the pilot , dispatcher, performance engineer, or operations planner can be groups into five categories , such as:

1. Maximize the distance traveled for a given amount of fuel (i.e. maximum range).

2. Minimize the fuel used for given distance covered (i.e. minimum trip fuel).

3. Minimize total trip time (i.e. minimum time).

4. minimize total operating cost for the trip (i.e. minimum cost, or economy speed).

5. Maintain the flight schedule . The first two objectives are essentially the same because in both cases the airplane will be flown to achieve optimum feel mileage.

In addition to one of the overall strategic objectives for cruise flight, pilots are often forced to deal with shortage term constraints that may require them to temporarily abandon their cruise strategy one or more times during a flight. These situations may include:

Flying a fixed speed that is compatible with other traffic on a specified route segment. Flying aseed calculated to achieve a required time of arrival at a fix. Flying a speed calculated to achieve minimum fuel flow when holding (i.e. maximum endurance). And when directed to maintain a specified speed by a air traffic control. Hence, when the air plane faced with a low fuel situation at destination, many pilits will opt to fly LRC speed, thinking that it will give them , the most miles from their remaining fuel. Also, if fuel prices increase relative to other costs, a corresponding reduction in CI will maintain the most economics operation of the air plane. If however an airline experience rising hourly costs, an increase in CI will retain the most economical operation . For this reason, flight crews typically reserve a recommend CI value from their flight operations department, and it is generally not advisable to deviate from this value unless specific short term constraints demand it.

How it can help air planes to execute for maximum fuel savings efficiently? For example, but times have clearly changed. Jet fuel prices have increased over times from 1990 to 2008 year. At this time, fuel is about 40% oa a tycpical airline's total operating cost. As a results airlines are reviewing all phases of flight to determine how fuel burn savings can be gained in each phase and in totel.

Boeing 777-200 extended range and 747-400 and (long-range, e.g. short range e.g. 717, medium range, e.g. 737-800 with winglate commercail air planes can impact fuel usage. However, flap setting must be appropriate for the situation to ensure air plane safely. Higher flap setting configurations use more fuel than low flags configurations.

The difference is small, but at today's prices the savings can be substantial especially for air planes that fly a light number of cycles each day. Hence, top fuel conservsation strategies for flight crews include: Take only the fuel you need, minimize the use of the nuxiliary power unit, taxi use efficiencly as possible, take off and climb efficiently , fly the air plane with minimum drag, choose routing carefully, strive to mantain optimum attitude, fly the proper cruise speed, descend at the appropriate point, configure in a timely manner.

Fuel conservation is a significant concern of every airline . An airline can choose an approach procedure and flap setting policy that was the least amount of fuel, but it should also consider the trade off involves with using this type of procedure.

Hence, Boeing flight crew can earn benefit, when they fly or air planes, such as to conserve fuel and reduce noise and emissions or to accommodate speed requests by air traffic control. All of these are fuel consumption reducing strategy to airlines.

● How airlines and airports implement successful netwpork strategies

What is airline network strategy ? Network management includes route planning, scheduling optimization, airline business planning and data analysis . How implement airline network strategy, airlines need to evaluate strengths and weaknesses of the current network strategy, identification of additional potential, recommendations for adjustments, network integration, due to merger or cooperation. Fleet and capacity evaluation , analysis of estimated passenger volume over time combined with option aircraft size and frequencies for current and potential future rotes / markets; competition response, modeling of results as an impact of competitor's action and reaction; establishing best practice network managment for new carriers include: route selection, network planning, scheduling, airline business planning includes forecasting of revenues and costs. Finally, any airlines need to establish network planning, such as network optimization and development, traffic and revenue forecasting, market -and -competitor analysis, scenarios for profit-optimized networks include: hub-strategies, evaluation of aliances, cooperation includes: route joint ventures in industry environment.

● Performance measurement system strategy

Any airlines may apply performance measurement methods to design the indicates of performance. Different models and frameworks are excellence models. Any airlines hope to achieve useful performance meaurement strategy. They need to answer these kep questions: Who are the key stakeholders and what they want and need? What strategy airlines have to put into place to satisfy the key stakeholders' want and need? What critical process do airlines need if they want to implement this strategy? What capability do they need to operate and improve this process? What does cost leadership strategy mean? Competitive price is decided for customer . Indoneasia, Malaysia , India and China countries are implementing, it can provide cheaper workforces and the cost of production will be covered.

In aviation service industry, cost strategy , it much relevant to be applied cost carrier, such as Vigin Blus, Ryanair Airways are implementing . However, some airlines combined the low cost carrier and full service

,which is known as low fare limited services.

Innovative marketing strategy is not only how to carry many more passengers, but also how to enable significant reduction in the costs of distribition and marketing. Such a strategy is used as a competitive strategy of low cost tariffs . For example, low cost focus strategy serve tourists or groups with certain destinations, e.g. the flights are carried out by certain airlines.

There are also tourist groups who travel to certain tourist destinations. Passengers only are transported be the tourist destinations, thus departure schedule won't be a basic need, lower price of ticket and flexible departure schedule as well as comfortable cabin are still the standard.

Another improvement of performance method, it is market orientation, it is believed to give psychological and social benefits to the employees , in the forms of greater pride and sense of belonging, as well as greater commitment to the organization.

Another strategy improves to service performance, it is distribution management strategy . Everyone can be brought benefits. It may achieve these benefits: Raising passenger numbers, as some airlines and airports are running at near full capacity. The effects of disruption are only becoming compounded. Social media can help airlines and airports to tackle dissuption management and avoid damaging their reputation with consumers.

So, when discuption is solved. It can help airports reduce discuption cost and damaging their reputation with consumers . Innovation may include: airlines attempt to develop standard procedure for common disruption situations, responding to regulations, such as the delay rule and compensation for cancellations with faster, more proactive decisions, collaborating with air traffic control facilities, airports, themselves views of resources, identify available options.

● What factors influence cost-related management quality ?

Thus, the reduction of costs lies at the core of the low cost airline model, which aims to offer lower fares, elimating some comfort and services that were traditionally quaranteed, e.g. employed to refer to low-cost flight. The use of an airline booking system, the suppression of free-in-flight catering, the use of secondary airports connected through a point-to-point network, and the use of homogeneous fleets are only a part of the innovative choices made by low-cost airlines. However, these are main important factors to influence route structure, type and characteristics of the aircraft cost of labor and management quality . For example, if the airline's pilot, airline passenger service people, cleaners , all salaries can be reduced to employ. Then, the airport or airline's labor cost will be reduced and it can influence it's air ticket price to be also decreased.

When the airline's air tickets price reduces, it will bring competitive low air ticket sale price to win other airline competitors more easily. How air ticket sale attractive prices ? The airline's air plane type and characteristics,, whether they ae comfortable to let passengers catch in their whole trip time. Whether their air planes are new or old model ? Whether their air planes' facilities can satisfy passengers entertainment need, e.g. chair can be bed to let passengers to sleep, television or movie is attractive to watch, music is soft sound etc. psychological entertainment facilities can let the airline passengers feel satisfactory or not.

Final view is management quality, such as whether the airline or airport CEO's management ability performance is either excellent or good or general or poor . They can influence whole airline or airport front -line service staffs' service performance to let passengers or airport visitors feel their services can satisfy their needs when they choose to catch the airline air planes to fly to the country to travel or work, but the country's airport staffs' service performances and airport facilities will influence their revisiting to the country's airport or rebuying the airline's air tickets again.

The final strategy is flying route strategy. I believe that whether the flying route is attractive or not, it can influence passengers to choose the airline preference. Which factors determine choice of flights on the Dhaka-London route? How could the airline be able to cope with the competitive advantages of its major rivals in this flying route? How is the competitive environment for airlines operating in this route? How could the airline sustain its competitive advantage and what can it do to gain more market share in this route?

A successful and attractive flying route design needs to amend and adjust its flying route design strategies and capabilities as the airline firm goes through its flying route design life cycle, when changes in passenger's flying route choice preferences. Hence, any airline needs to know whether what its SWOT (strengths, weaknesses, opportunities, threats) before it decides to implement which flying route(s). Because manay flying routes choicew will be influenced by its current SWOT environment situation. For organization of new flying route to the UK airport from UK , e.g. London ciry airport, the HK airline needs to know whether what its strengths , e.g. customer loyalty, its strengths can provide the most rapid . The most cheapest, the more comfortable flying feeling from HK airport flys to UK London airport or from UK , London city airport flys to HK airport, its UK , London city flying route can provide competitive fare al promotion, extra baggage allowance, airline brand image , whether is famous to UK travellers, providing online seats reservation for any UK , London flights services, airline organization size and airline brand , whether it can get travelling passegners, loyalty or confidence either to fly to UK , London city from UK city airport, or flying to HK city from UK, London city airport, providing regular UK , London flying route schedule, network presence how much UK flying route cost cutting, Uk air planes' aircrafts facilities whether are enough to satisfy HK or UK to catching the airline's air planes flying entertainment needs. Does it one new route development opportunity of direct flughts from HK airport to UK , London city airport. HK air port has enough terminals number to let facilities to provide passengers stay in HK airport when UK , London city travellers arrive HK airport? Does HK airport lacks technologica facilities to satisfy new UK , London city airport flying route development , e.g. providing enough spaces to let air fleets stay in HK airport, aircraft manintenance whether is enough? Does HK airport encounter shortages of experienced front line counter service staffs to serve UK , London city travellers in airport? When the seasonal time is holiday travelling time for UK visitors, is UK new flying route rising fuel cost? Does new entrants to develop another UK , London city flying route from HK? Has new UK , London city from HK flying route , these weaknesses , such as lacking enough resource to develop another another new flying route or no direct flight or long hour flight after the HK airline developed the new UK , London city flying route to the HK airline from HK airport. Has new Uk, London city flying route development enountered these threats: strong competiton, high interest and UK foreign currency exchange rates, raising fuel cost, economic recession decline in the UK airline industry, environmental pollution etc. issues influence UK travellers choose to travel to HK desires. So, SWOT analysis must be needed to consider in order to develop any new flying route in order to avoid servious high cost expenditure loss to any airlines.

So, above these tangible , e.g. fuel cost control , route choice, network cooperation choice and intangible, e.g. service performance factors can influence whether the airline's network cooperation strategy, route choice strategy or low cost strategy can succeed or fail. So, airlines or airports can not neglect these factors to be revised in order to achieve any strategies in success more easily.

CHAPTER THREE

Airport service performance satisfactory strategy

Airline employee positive emotion method

Emotional labor factor

Airline service industry, front line travelling passengers service workers' emotional challenge concerns cabin crew and airline ground service employee whose service quality or performance how to serve travelling passengers in order to reach service level or satisfy their service performance needs to be accepted. So, how to influence airline service labour individual emotional matter which will be one major factor to let travelling passengers how they feel satisfactory to the airline service.

The question concerns how to let airline service cabin crews and air ground service employees build long term good emotion to serve their airline travelling passengers. Because bad emotional airline service labors will damage the whole airline employers' loyalty as well as reducing travelling passengers number in possible.

Will a lot stresses at work cause bad emotion to airline ground service employees? The hospitality industry comprises of travel and tourism and the major segments include lodgings and cuisines (hotels, restaurants), transport(airlines, rentals, cruise and railway companies), travel and tour operators. All of these related travelling industries' employees , they are emotional labor, whose service performance or service attitude will influence future potential travelling passengers' airline choices to the airline operating servicer again. Any airline service employees in these service sector industries, have to interact with their travelling clients, be its customers on a regular emotion reflecting basis. So, they must be patient to listen any travelling passengers' enquires in order to help them to solve any problems considerably.

Emotional labor is managing one's feelings to generate a publicly accepted facial and bodily display of emotion. Emotional labor is an expression of emotion for a wage. Jobs involve face to face or voice to voice interactions with clients (travelling passengers), jobs demanding the employee to produce and alter an emotional state in other person, and jobs allowing the employer to implement certain amount of control over the emotional activities of the employees, produce or create emotional labor among the employees.

Thus, long time bad emotional airline front labors number increasing, it will influence the airline whole service member performance to be its airline passengers. However, many airline organizations have their owning set of norms or policies that determine these feeling rules. These are specially seen in customer service industries. IN long term, these strict policies will let airline front service staffs feel stress or pressure, because they won't feel to be punished in possible, e.g. without salary continue increasing, dismissal (lose jobs), changing to another position to do more simple or boring job duties, if they are discovered that their working service performances are not satisfied to their airline employers in any time.

So, strict airline organizational policies will be one strict or pressure emotional regulation to any airline front service staffs. This emotional regulation refers to a person's capability to accept and understand his or her experience of emotions to get involved in healthy strategies in managing emotions which are uncomfortable whenever required, when they need to contact their airline passengers every day. In fact, it has possible that they will accept unreasonable complaint from their airline passengers, even they perform very good or they have help their airline passengers to solve any enquiries when they feel any needs, they stay in airports any time. So, it has close relationship among airline front service staffs' emotions and the airline's policy as well as their service attitude. Thus, good airline policy will build good airline service staffs' emotions and good service attitude or service behaviour to serve their airline passengers every day in possible.

Any airline organizations can not neglect to consider how to build (keep) good airline front labor emotion issue. Because they are any airlines' representatives, if they can build good
images to let the airline the airline passengers to feel. Then, it will influence many airline passengers to choose to buy the airline tickets to replace

other airlines because they like its front airline front staffs' services. SO, any airline organizations need to consider front service staffs' health status and definite psychological or mental diseases more than physical diseases, because many airline front service staffs only need to serve their airline passengers and they do not need to move any heavy things in airports in general. They need to spend more time to contract their passengers more than any things. When their passengers give their passports or/and any related travelling documents, e.g. air tickets to them to check in to find whether they can allow to enter airport restrict areas, and if they give their luggage to them, they also need to help them to measure its size and weight heavy to decide whether they need to pay extra fee and their luggage are permitted either to keep to them together to enter the air planes to fly or separate air planes to fly to destination. So, they need to make accurate judgement need to avoid any error occurrence. They do not allow to do any wrong judgement or error in order to be complain by their airline passengers often. Hence, any airline organizations need have good method to help their airline front service staffs to avoid to do any wrong judgements in order to influence any flights delay or customers' complaints , due to their personal wrong judgement to their passengers cause in possible.

Thus, any airline organizations require to enquire themselves these questions: Is there any influence of emotional labor (surface acting and deep acting) on the general mental health or psychological disease of airline employees? Is these any difference in the experience of emotional labor across demographics (age/gender/mental status/work experience of airline employees influence their service performance? Because above any one factors , such as every airline front service staff individual age, airline service experience, marital status of these factors will influence their emotions to be good or bad to serve their airline passengers every day. Hence , any airline organizations need to investigate every airline front service employee individual background in order to arrange the most suitable policy to train their front line or ground airline service staffs' skill in order to let them to feel less stress or pressure
or they can feel happy to enjoy to serve their airline passengers.

On conclusion, reducing airline front or ground service staffs' psychological stress or mental pressure issue which will be the most effective or the best solution to assist them to raise confidence to serve their airline passengers in airports in long time. I believe that it is the most rapid psychological solution method to assist any one airline front or ground service staff to raise service level in short time.

Airports service environment factor

The environment of airports service environment for the airline services, which will also influence travelling passengers' travelling destinations and travelling frequent times choices. The airport price factor includes income growth, aviation technology and local economic / geographical features of the country's domestic or overseas airports both. IN fact, airports, airports are indeed two sides businesses, it has commercial relationship between both airlines and passengers. So, airports' pricing will influence passengers' travelling demands to the airlines in the country. Any countries' airport(s) need(s) to respond how to help themselves country airlines how to increase passengers number and airlines choices in order to achieve attracting traffic on frequent air planes flying aim. Because the country's travelling passengers number increases , it will influence the country's airport(s) ' income increases indirectly, instead of the countries' any airlines themselves incomes.

Hence, any country's airport(s) will be one good platform to let travelling passengers to stay in the country's airport(s). It means that id the country's airport(s) can build good service image and reasonable products sale price and comfortable shopping environment to attract any countries' passengers feel comfortable and worth to stay in themselves countries' airport(s), when they need to transfer air planes to stay in the country's airport, e.g. one hour to five hours short time, even overnight long time staying. However, if they

feel the country's airport(s) are(is) more comfortable and clean to stay, less noise, as well as they have enough chairs to let them to sit or sleep and large area to let them to work in the airport ground floor.

Moreover, the country's airport(s) can have enough restaurants , bookshops, any electronic or other kinds product shop[s, even cinema etc. shopping or entertainment services to satisfy

the passengers whose eating needs, entertainment needs, shopping needs in the airport. Then, I believe that the country's airport(s) can help itself airlines to attract many passengers

to choose to increase travelling times to the country frequently. For example, when the country's airport passengers feel that the airport restaurant food concessionaires will probably provide enjoy positive external gains from having more flights at the airports, additional or better eating facilities are unlikely to provide external benefits to the airlines by stimulating many more passengers with local origins or destinations to use the airport. I believe these airport restaurants can influence the choices of transit passengers whether which country will be their transfer air plane's short journey staying airport destination to fly to their final destinations. Although, transit passengers usually stay to the transfer air plane airport in short time, but they hope that these any one transit staying airport can have any restaurants to provide good taste food to them to eat when they feel hungry, if the transfer air plane country's airport can provide enough restaurants and they can have different food taste choice and reasonable price. Then, the airport's restaurants may attract many short time transit passengers to choose to eat their food, even many passengers will like to choose the country's airline to buy tickets to stay short time to wait to transfer another air plane to fly to their final destination to replace another country's airport to stay short time.

Hence, it seems that any countries' airports' entertainment, eating and shopping service environment will influence any countries transit passengers whether they ought either choose to stay short time this country's airport in prefer or another country's airport to stay short time in prefer in order to decide to buy the country's airline air ticket for transfer airplane to another destination. Hence, any airports service environment will influence any countries passengers how to make transit airport destination short time staying choice.

However, I also suggest that an airport will place a lower revenue -over cost burden on that side of the travelling market that benefits the other the most. Assuming one passenger can earn benefit enjoyed by airlines from an extra- passenger using the airport, the airlines will be willing to pay up to this amount to increase passenger enjoyed benefit feeling.

The airport can extract rent from the airlines up to above their allocated costs for providing the airport short time staying platform (transfer air plane short time staying airport) for eating, entertainment, shopping need service of increasing their destination arriving passengers or transfer another air plane passengers number base. This involves transferring the external benefits derived by airlines from additional passengers using the transfer airport to the another destination airport.

On the another view, from a airport location choice perspective, locating or expanding an airport near a city center can reduce or at least contain passenger access costs . But, because land is like to be more expensive, the airside costs to airlines are serious higher and if the various other external costs of aviation are included. Hence, countryside or the airport is built far away from city center in the country. This location is one reasonable location choice, because it can reduce noise to influence people who are living when air planes are often flying or landing on the airport and the rent cost to the airport's any business renters will be influenced to reduce. Then, their food , product or entertainment service prices charge to the airport consumers will also be reduced. Thus, any airports ought nor neglect their building location choices in any countries because they will influence airport business renters sale prices.

Lean maintenance repair and manual
error factor

Any airlines must need air plans to catch passengers to fly to travel. So, any air plans will need often to fly. Every flight will need long time to fly, e.g. short trip needs to fly less than five hours, even long trip needs to fly more than five hours, even ten hours. If many passengers choose the country to travel, the air plan needs to fly
frequently to catch every flight passengers to go to the travelling destination frequently. So, any airlines air plans often need to check whether they have any engine machines has broken, need to be repaired in possible in order to let passengers feel the airline air plans are safe. If the airline's any air plans have occurred any accidents when they are flying, even the accidents cause any one passengers hurt, even death. Then, these flying accidents will let passengers feel life risk to choose this airline's any air plans to catch to fly. IN special, long time trip(s) flight(s). So, lean maintenance and engine check is needed to consider for any one airplane to any airline in order to improve efficiencies and minimize costs, maintenance, repair,
and overhaul services in the aviation industry sector, even avoiding any flying accident occurrence or reducing serious flying accidents occurrence chance to bring any one passenger
hurt, even death when they are catching any one of the airline air plans to travel. Thus, any one of airline safety is one important successful factor to any airlines.

Instead of passenger safety aspect, the flying logistics safety factor is also important. The central tenet of the lean to a flying process can mainfest in a variety of ways , as over stalled
and underused inventory and misallocated labour, time transportation and

logistics. From a customer's perspective, value-added activities are necessary and customers are willing to pay for activities(Bamber, 2000, Glass, 2016). For example, improvements caused by lean introduction in aviation industry in order to avoid misallocated labour time, increasing number of old broken tools, and obsolute jigs and fixtures. Aviation MRO services have been reported by the MIT Lean Aerospace Initiative (2005) to result in:

(1) Set up time: 17 to 85 percent improvement.

(2) Lead time: 16 to 50 percent improvement.

(3) Labour hours: 10 to 71 percent improvement.

(4) Cost: 11 to 50 percent improvement.

(5) Productivity: 27 to 100 percent improvement.

(6) Cycle time: 20 to 97 percent improvement.

(7) Airline airplane manufacturing factory floor space: 25 to 81 percent improvement.

(8) Travel distance (people and products): 42 to 95 percent improvement.

(9) Airplanes engine inventory or work in progress: 31 to 98 percent improvement.

(10) Scape, rework , deflects or inspection: 20 to 80 percent improvement.

Hence, any airlines' airplanes need to be achieve any one of above improvement at least percent level in order to keep airplane's accident occurrence chance to the least level.

Moreover, airplanes' pilot employees their flying experiences or flight numbers factor is also important to influence airplane safe flying issue. Because if the pilot has less flying

expereince or he is not proficient pilot, or his flight number is less. This pilot's individual flying factor will also influence the airplan's safety when he is driving the airplane.

So, any airlines need to consider how to train any one of pilot to be one proficient pilot, because id less experienced pilot , he/she is not proficient to drive any one airplane to fly. Then, the flying accident occurrence chance will also raise. It is one critical successful factor to influence passengers' confidence to choose the airline's airplanes to catch, instead of maintenance repair and checking engines factor.

On conclusion, raising travelling passengers' safe confidences factor will be one critical successful factor to influence any airlines' services level, because flying safety issue

must be one important matter to be considered to any passengers when they decide to choose the airline's airplane to catch to fly to any destinations. If one airline can not guarantee any flying accidents won't occur, to cause any passengers hurt or death. Then, any passengers won't have confidence to feel its others services level can satisfy their basic flying enjoyment

needs. Due to passengers' life cost must be no worth calculation more than other service cost. When they choose to catch the airlines' any one airplane to fly to the another destination form the

country's airport. Hence, the influence of human factor in airport maintenance factor will influence any airlines' services feeling level to their passengers because human factor is one of the safety barrier which is used in order to prevent accidents or incidents of aircraft.

Therefore, the question is to which extent the error caused by human factor is included into the share of errors that are made during aircraft maintenance, such as flying

accidents, incidents, injuries, death, damages related to aircraft operation and maintenance. More airlines' detailed analyses have led to the knowledge that it is necessary to study the

interrelation of repair people, machines, airline factory maintenance and manufacturing working environment, and the air planes production processes. Human is the key factor production

process and in the process of operation of technical means since gives new value to the object of any one airplane manufacturing process.

As a factor, the human is not perfect and introduces unintentional error in the system. It is important to develop a system of ever identification and to work constantly on error

prevention. The works and activities on aircraft maintenance can produce hidden and active errors on the aircraft. Hidden errors are a type of errors that are seemingly invisible during aircraft

flying. Active errors are errors that occur immediately and result in immediate aircraft damage or injury , even death to any travelling passengers.

Hence, non human or without human factors will be less number to compare human factors to cause any flying incidents or accidents occurrence easily, e.g. damaging engine, old engine (no renew engine), fire, crash etc. different kinds of causes. However, the main causes of human errors to cause any flying accidents may include: lack of communication between the pilot(s) and airport airplane landing staffs, complacency (assessment of work according to previous working experience), lacking of flying knowledge to the pilot, distraction, lack of

team work, fatigue, lack of materials and technological support), pressure on the work performer, lack of assertiveness (lack of self-confidence or technical approach to work),stress (working under pressure), lack of awareness etc. different human factors. Any one of above human factors will influence any flying accidents cause.

Moreover, instead of human factor, the flying working environment which refers to the space and place for work as well as the conditions of work factor will also influence human

error occurrence increasing chance, e.g. time pressure, equipment and tools enough number supplies, night shift, all of any one work environment factor will also influence human error

occurrence increasing chance in any flight flying. However, the factors that lead to cause of maintenance error may be caused from wrong information system supplies of equipment , aircraft

manufacturer, wrong working equipment and tools, wrong design of aircraft equipment and parts, incorrect working task arrangement, lacking technical education to the aircraft maintenance

workers, employee's bad personality, poor aircraft factory manufacturing working environment, poor airline company organization structure, working management and control and poor

communication etc. different manual or non manual factors.

Hence, all of above any one non manual factors will also raise manual error factor to cause any flying accidents occurrence chances. However, if any airlines hope to satisfy their passengers' flying service level. They must consider non manual and manual both factors for aircraft lean maintenance repair service aspect.

Influence of airside and off airport to airport geographical choice factor

What does airport airside means ? It includes a system of three components: runways, taxiways and agron-gate areas, on which aircraft and aircraft support vehicles operate. It brings this questions: Why can airport airside operation influence passengers feeling to the country's airport and airline services? How does it influence airport ground service staffs' service performance?

In fact, this airside airport physical area choice has direct relationship between aircraft and apron gate areas of the terminal processing of passenger and cargo. They are major factors to influence operations on runway component. It means that airport ground service staffs' service efficiency, used for the passengers and air fright catching any airplanes processing.

Hence, in a geographical sense, landside and airside capacity on how designing and building og geographical area can bring indirect influence to passengers. They need to enter or indirect influence the airport , in special, many flights are staying on the airport runway as well as many passengers need to leave from the airplanes or enter to the airplanes in the same time on the airport boundary. Hence, if the airport has good airside design , then many passengers will feel convenient to leave or enter the airport from the airside areas.

Airports are perhaps truly intermodel terminals in the transportatoin system. They provide an intersafe among air highway, rail and even water way travel. They are an important part of the medium and long distance intercity transportation system in our future transportation tools. Hence, it has enough reasons to support airside geographical airside and off airport factors can influence an airport and its airline flying service providers on its capacity as well as how it's capacity can influence passengers' satisfactory level when they arrive the country's airport. Hence, airport's congestion growth problem that is needed to consider to any airports because when one airport 's congestion is growing.

It will influence passengers service satisfactory level to be fallen down in possible, e.g. capacity is increased by the addition of a new access road, such as additions provide a major increase.Thus, the stair step growth, it will cause congestion growth because if the airport had used many areas for stair step growth and passengers will have less space to let them to walk on the ground and their airport congestion feeling will also increase when passengers are staying to leave the airport or waiting for check in or check out or waiting to transfer another airplane in the country's airport.The major airside factors to influence travelling passengers whose airport service feeling may include as below:

Availability of enough land for expansion for runways, availability of aids to navigation and air traffic control techniques that could result in reduction of separation between aircraft , noise, aircraft mix, load factor, exclusive use and use of gates , enough airside and outside facilities, availability of airspace, whether aircraft large size is enough capacity and where is location of gates, staffing, equipment freight, environmental protection regulation, and community attitudes toward airside operation.

Thus, whether the airport has enough facilities to satisfy passengers staying in its airport service need, it will have indirect influence further passengers increasing or decreasing number problem. For example, if the airport terminal functions are spread over a large geographic area, access and facilities have to be expanded to accommodate the spread-out configuration of the terminal or if terminal facilities are grouped together, the access facilities can be congregated into a smaller geographical area.

The capacity of the landside is a function of the terminal design , which has a major influence on the relative to between airside and landside capacity. Also, these off airport factors can also influence landside capacity, they may include: off airport parking, off airport terminals, urban development pattern, multiple jurisdiction, financial resources etc. issues. The sub factors of the off-airport access functions , they can influence passengers' services feeling to the airport. They may include: user and vehicle characteristics, e.g. occupants per vehicle, separate and preferential guide way subsystems, roadway traffic management, access link to major transportation , transportation connections. All of these airside and off-airport facilities will

influence passengers' servicing feeling when they arrive any countries' airports. Hence, any countries' airports ought not neglect any one of these minor airside facilities of inside airports to outside airports both.

The another geographical choice airport building issue, it is also one critical factor for how the development of airport cities. It will influence passengers' service feeling to any country airport. The questions may include: Why may any country need to develop an airport city? Can it bring economic benefit and attract many passengers to choose to travel the country? Can the airport city reform to raise airport service performance or service level? Airports have become new dynamic centers of economic activity, incorporating several commercial and

entertainment services inside passenger terminals, when developing a hotels and accommodations , office complexes, conference and exhibition centers or leisure facilities choices for leisure passengers and business passengers both.

Airport-centered development may occur at different spatial scales (from the micro scale of the passenger terminal to the regional or metropolitan scale), thus assuming different shapes and mainfestations. Different concepts to address these developments can be found in the " airport city", airport corridor, and aerotopolis (Guller, M. & Guller, M, 2003).

I shall explain how airport city concept can help to raise passenger service performance feeling in airports and airlines as below:

In general, airport passengers hope airports ought provide these different kinds service and achievement the lowest satisfactory service quality or performance level to let

them to feel, such as air transport needs have complex airport -neighborhood interactions (in what concerns an eventual development towards the concept of airport city) requires the

identification of thes takeholders involved and an awareness of the relationships between them. Any airport's main task needs to provide traveling, air transport, shipping, entertainment services to the dual market of airlines and travelers. As such, its primary interaction consists of the supply and demand relationship with the users stakeholder group (passengers and airlines), which results in broad terms in the airports aeronautical revenues. Furthermore, non-aeronautical (commercial) revenues also result from the interactions between airport and users, namely from agents such as cargo and passengers oriented organizations who pay rents or concession feeling to the airport authority, depending on the commercial arrangements binding these agents.

Thus, one successful airport city, it ought provide good neighborhood transport service to travelling passengers, e.g. bus, taxi, ferry etc. public transportation service. It aims to avail any airport passengers can catch any one of these public transportation tools to arrive airport or leave the airport easily. It also needs to provide hotel, conference service for business visitors as well as retail shops, cinemas for shopping visitors or entertainment visitors when they are staying in the country's airport(s). Also, it ought provide facilities to any cargo -oriented organizations to deliver any cargo in short time rapidly. So, one airport's any neighborhood facilities have relationship to influence any passengers and airport organizations' service performance feeling between different user agents including: service provision (e.g. between passengers and businesses), business transactions, supply and demand (e.g. between public transport providers and passengers and passengers or visitors) and employer-employee relationships (businesses and workforce , such as airport airline ground service workers). Because if they feel that they can work in one comfortable airport working environment, they will feel happy and enjoyable to serve their passengers more everyday. It means that any airports' facilities will have indirect relationship to influence airport ground service workers' psychology to feel either enjoyable or hate to work in the airport environment often.

On conclusion, airports ought need to consider themselves airside and off airport facilities whether they have enough supplies and innovate their facilities to be better , even perfect in order to satisfy any airport visitors, travelers, user organizations and airport ground service employees to enjoy to work and use their services if they hope their service level or performance is satisfied to their service needs for long term.

Influencing air connectivity to service quality factor

Can air connectivity growth decreases travel costs for attracting travelling passengers, consumers and businesses and facilities global productive growth? This seems to be particularly an issue when airport capacity is scare or when new airports are added to an existing airport system. What is air connectivity ?

Why does air connectivity raise passengers services? How to measure air connective service?

When direct and indirect connectivity relate to the airport connectivity available to local travelling passengers, any airports ought need to raise extra

airline services to raise service quality , e.g. cheaper air ticket price, in-flight service extra service provision, e.g. comfortable and clean and quiet air port waiting environment

service provision and feeling. However, passengers will generally prefer direct, non-stop connections over indirect air connectivity service.

Air connectivity service can assist airlines to raise competitive effort an offer and they provide access to the many destinations with too little demand for a direct flight, such as minimum connecting time differs in quality , due to in-flight time differences, the inconvenience and risk of missing a connection and transfer time for direct or indirect flights. Hence, any airlines can reduce passengers indirect or direct flight in-flight time to wait airplanes arrive to catch when they arrive any airports. This air in flight waiting time shorten service will attract many passengers to choose the airline to catch airplanes if its inflight waiting time to airport passengers is lesser than other airlines' in-flight waiting time in any airports. It can raise airline service quality, due to the airline has many passengers feel in-flight waiting time is shorten than other airlines often.

In fact, airport connectivity is one good concept method to raise passengers' satisfactory service level. One of the important factors for the connectivity of airports may include: The size and economic strength of the local catchment area how drives outbound demand, size and economic activities as well as tourism attractiveness are an important cariable factor in explaining inbound demand (including the propensity to flying demand), landside accessibility drives the size of the catchment area that airlines can serve from a particular airport within a certain landside travel time, apart from the socio-economic variables factor, also cultural , political and the historical ties play a role in explaining demand the origin-destination level factor. All of the research on the factors that explain air level, demand at the origin-destination or airport level is widespread, including gravity modelling (e.g. a bed at al., 2001) and regressions on aggregate

airport demand (Dobruszkes, 2011). All of any one factors may be airport connectivity service to influence passengers' service feeling level in airports and airlines both service quality.

ON airport visit costs aspect, airlines also need to consider airport visit costs in their route development strategy. Visit costs may also influence passenger choice behavior when

airlines pass on higher/lower charges to the passenger through air fares. Although, airport visit costs generally represent a limited share of an airline's total operational costs, this share can be more significant for short haul flights as well as fair airlines. All of any one these airport charges and passenger fees variable may influence passengers airlines choice. They may include:

Fees variable, landing charge, parking charge for their vehicles or aircraft, passenger luggage charge, security charge, boarding bridge charge, noise charge, emission charge, airport development service increasing charge, check -in charge, terminal charge, cargo charge. So, if any one of these charges influence the airline ticket price rises, it will influence passengers' air ticket purchase choice to the airline in possible.

On airport service levels aspect, for keeping and attracting passengers, airlines and airports need to compete with services that improve the passengers experience. Such service

factors concern for immigration and luggage, but also relate to the terminals, waiting transfer another air plane time, shopping facilities, toilets, atmosphere and space cleaniness, friendliness of staff and availability of delicated lounges. Together they determine the image of an airport and its perceived value by passengers and airlines.

On airline routes development aspect, it can also influence passengers choices to the airline, e.g. Australia airline had developed long route to England destination. Any Australia

passengers can fly to England route directly. They do not need to transfer another air plane to go to England. Although, flying time is above 12 hours long time, but it can bring available to

passengers. They do not need to spend time to wait another air plane to transfer to go England in Australia any airports. THus, airline route development strategy airline planners require detailed, accurate information to make new route decisions, but airlines usually do not have the resources to fully evaluate every new route market. So, they need a sound well articulated business case, can convince airlines to introduce new air services, as well as airport / destinations can influence the airline planning process.

For example, Interviewer indicates that new routes are a huge investment and risk to an airline in airline economic view point, if the airline had not gathered any data to evaluate

whether the new route is worth to develop and predict passengers' new route choice behavior. It assumed 75% lead factor will influence any new route development in success. It indicates these different aircraft type and seats per flight, annual passenger requirements data for these aircrafts: Boeing 747 aircraft needs to satisfy 400 at least seats per flight and annual passenger requirement need 219, 000, aircraft airbus A340 aircraft needs 280 at least seats per flight and annual passenger requirements need 153,300 , Boesing 767 to 300 aircraft needs 220 at least seats per flight and annual passenger requirements need 120, 450 . Boeing 737 to 700 aircraft needs 76,650 and regional Jet aircraft needs 100 at least seats per flight and annual passenger requirements need 54,750.

Hence, any airlines need have route priorities strategy before they decide which new flight route(s) will be developed , in order to achieve airlines add service in order of expected profitability, different airlines have pursued different strategies, destinations can move up the priority board with: solid research and analysis (always) and incentives (sometimes).However, any airline questions for new routes may include as below:

What is the current, actual market for a potential route?
How much can my airline stimulate the flight flying market?
How will the competition react?
How much market share will achieve?
How will be the connectivity contribution?
Will the new route be a financial success?

Hence, any airlines need to reduce uncertainty and risk, before they decide to develop any new route market.

The air service development process may include as below:

Step one: market assessment, required a quantify the time size of the existing air travel market

step two: strategy, deficiency analysis and detailed route analysis

step three: business case analysis, packaging and presenting the information to airlines

step fourth: evaluate and negotiate airline incentives

It is the final steps an appropriate incentive, in certain circumstances, helps airlines commit to new air service to satisfy any new route passengers' more satisfactory flying needs.

Similarly, the strategy steps follow: benchmark air services, identify deficiencies, identify new route opportunities, identify potential air service providers, assess viability of potential air services and prioritize route opportunities and target carriers.

Any airlines may find any information concerns new route business cases to decide their countries flying new routes choice , such as: catchment area profile: demographics, economy, tourist etc. information, airport profile : traffic and facilities information market profile; market sizes , top city pairs, traffic leakage etc. information, suggested service : frequency , schedule, airport routing information, route analysis: market share, load factor, stimulation potential, self-diversion etc. information, any airlines' past flying routes strategic considerations etc. information in order to predict and evaluate whether how many further passenger number is flying that they accept to choose the new flying routes travelling needs.

Hence, how to design to impact either the supply or demand for any new flight routes that is only important because of the country has less number of passengers accept to choose the new flying route to fly. Then, the new flying route does not needed to be design to supply to the country's travelling passengers because their acceptance to this new flying route ends are very less. However, the demand level is low new flying route needs to satisfy these three qualifying services criteria, such as: Are new routes only? Increase on existing routes? Does it work service rent incentives? Will the new flying route be satisfied to air service to the airline passengers and airport waiting passengers, e.g. strategically important? Marginally (unprofitable) self-sustaining in the short term? New flying routes only? Increase an existing routes? Service rent incentives?

How can airports afford aggressive airline incentive / fee discounts and still fund route development marketing in a difficult economy? I recommend that the solution method may include new flying route design and developing and maximizing non-aeronautical revenue streams both, such as retail and duty free, food and beverage, parking , loyalty and premium programs and land development to airport building. Marketing funding strategy may be an ineffective incentive for travelling destinations. However, it may not differentiate a market, as route marketing incentives are used by over 80% of communities in the U.S. marketing incentives can be: Unilateral airport pays 100% or cooperative airlines matches some portion, funding amounts are often tied on the capacity of inbound seats to be available on the new flight (flying) route. By calculating the economic impact of new visitors (spend at the destination), a destination can calculate the return on investment in cooperative new flight (flying) route market.

On conclusion, air connectivity is one important factor to influence any country's travelling passengers to the airline's service quality or service level in order to achieve new flying (flight) route design , reducing inflight transfer another airplane waiting time in airport, or marketing development in success. So, any airlines can not neglect this air connectivity will influence their passengers' service quality. Hence, air connectivity factor is also very important to influence any travelling passengers' service satisfactory level.

How to measure and rise airline
service quality

How are airline performing ? Nowadays, the rise of the low cost airlines' competition is serious, due to airlines hope to rise themselves attractions to influence passengers to choose to use their travelling services. So, different airlines have spend long time to build their unique person-to-person passenger services, which passengers use of different airlines, e.g. digital electronic air tickets purchase method. Any airlines hope to make each journey personalized to the individual will gain market share and improve its service quality to be more unique in order to reach the efforts of airlines to build high levels of customer service appears to have been generally noticed by passengers, when they choose to buy the airline's digital electronic ticket or paper air ticket to use its flying service.

Hence, improvement their digital e-ticket purchase experience and communications factor, for example, if any passengers can enter the airline's air ticket purchase website to buy electronic ticket to pre-book seats in the short time rapidly as well as there are enough seats number to supply to them to pre-book. So, they do not need to worry about without any seats to supply to them to catch the airline's flight to fly to anywhere in any time available conveniently. So, it seems that there is plenty of space for airlines to grow and improve their digital experience and communication method to let any passengers to feel, if the airline hopes to let its passengers to feel that it has unique service to compare others airlines.

The aviation industry plays a major role in the aspect of work and leisure to passengers around the global. So, nowadays passengers' demands to any airlines' service quality had been raised. Hence, any airline service industry messengers are under pressure to prove their services are customers oriented service improvement of performance that guarantees competitive advantages to the global travelling marketplace. So, it also implies that any airlines' services performance will be influenced to cause many passengers feel more poor and let passengers dissatisfy the airline's service performance. The, the airline will possible lose many passengers, due to passengers have many airlines choices, they can find any airlines to replace which any one airline to buy air ticket from internet at home immediately.

However, airlines' comfortable seats arrangement service provision feeling factor is still important in preferable to compare other factors, because passengers must need to sit any seats in any air planes. So, whether the air plane can provide new comfortable seats to let passengers to feel this factor is still the most important factor to influence any passengers to choose to the airline's air plane to catch. For example, service comfortability is how passengers observed the quality of service offered them by the airline's cleanliness, quiet zone, shops, restaurants and business pavilion in functioning like staffs, information desk, and in flight announcement are included as tangible features by the passengers (Geraldine et a.,2013). All of these factors are needed often to measure whether their service performances are satisfactory to themselves passengers service needs.

Moreover, the other factors may include service affordability , it can be regarded as given passenger the opportunity to select from inclusive air ticket prices made available to the different group of passengers by the airlines, as a gesture of goodwill , to establish and reinforce customer loyalty and repeat purchases essential for the airline continuity as well as service reliability. it is the probability that airline will carry out its expected function satisfactory as stated in the flight schedule. Hence, there is a strong link between different airlines' service quality variables, airline image and repeat patronage from the passengers.

Service quality is a measure of how well the service level delivered matches passengers expectations to measure service quality based on input from focus groups. It consists of five factors (tangibles, reliability, responsiveness, assurance and empathy). All of these factors will be identifies that how the airline service quality can be satisfactory to its passengers ' psychological and emotion enjoyable service needs.

Any one of these any five service factors will be important to influence the airline's passengers service feeling level to the airline. It means that the passenger will have more chance to choose the airline's service again (repeating purchase its air ticket). Hence, any airlines can not neglect any one of service feeling to its passengers. It needs often to enquire questionnaires to evaluate whether its these five aspects of service quality , if it discovered any of these five aspects of service level is poor, e.g. 5 scale is the best service performance level, then it can attempt to find its error whether which aspects, it needs to very need to reach the 5 scale , the best service performance level when many passengers feel, e.g. enquiring 100 passengers who give 5 scale to reliability service aspect, before reliability service aspect has less than 50% passengers from 100 passengers who feel the airlines concerns this reliable service level aspect questions to be the best. It is one kind of measurement service quality method to any airlines.

Other service performance evaluation factor is satisfaction in the job to every airline front service or ground service staffs to the airline. Job satisfaction describes how content an employee is with his or her job. It is how the employee responses to a job. It can be considered as a part of life satisfaction to one organization, when the employee is working in the organization. Hence, if one airline front service as ground service staff who can feel more job satisfaction to compare his/her prior airline employer. Then, he/she won't be easy to change his/her present airline employer.

However, some factors can influence job satisfaction are pay and benefit, fair performance appraisal, career and promotional opportunities, proper reward and recognition, work-family life balance, the job itself, proper working conditions, leadership chance, autonomy in work.

Job satisfaction can also involve complex number of variables, circumstances, opinions and behavioral tendencies and a variety of work related outcomes, such as commitment, involvement, motivation, satisfaction, attendance. Hence, any airlines also need to concern how let their employees feel job satisfaction issue in order to avoid their leaving turnover number increases, due to job satisfaction and dissatisfaction depend on the expectations what the job supplies for an employee not the nature of the job.

Finally, instead of concerning employees job satisfaction issue, any airlines also need to concern passengers satisfaction issue because it will have any passengers will choose the airline, if it can bring more service satisfaction to let them to feel , then they will become repeat passengers to the airline.

What kinds of factors passengers were looking for and what were the reasons of choosing a specific airline? When one airline often is complained from its passengers. It will have more mistakes to let them to feel or dissatisfy its service. Hence the airlines needs to find which are its mistakes and improve in order to satisfy its passengers' expectations, e.g. finding what are the mistakes to the airlines' serious concern regarding passenger complaints and complaint satisfaction in order to make the airline more likely to meet its passengers' expectation in case of a problem. Hence, any airlines need to concern how to improve its employees' satisfactory service as well as its passengers' satisfactory service both issues as well as how to measure their service quality whether is enough to achieve general service acceptable performance to its passengers.

Reference

A bed, S. Y. A.O. Ba-Fail and S.M. Jasimuddin (2001), " An economatic analysis of international air travel demand in Saudi Arabia". Journal of air transport managmement, vol. 7, pp.143-148.

Bamber, L., & Dale, B.G. Lean production : a study of application in a traditoinal manufacturing environment. Production planning & control, 11 (3), 291-298, 2000.

Dobruszkes, F.M. Lennert and G. Van Hamme (2011). " An analysis of the determinants of air traffic volume for European metropolitan area". Journal of transport geographyy, vol. 19/4/pp.755-762.

Gealdine, O., & David , U.C. (2013). effects of airline service quality on airline image and passengers' loyalty: Findings from Arill Air Nigeria passengers, Journal of hospitality and management tourism, 4(2), 19-28. doi: http://dx.doi: 10.5897/HMT 2013, 0089.

Glass, R., Seifermann, S., & Metternich, J. The spread of lean production in the assembly, Process and maching industry. Procedia CIRP, 55, 278-283, 2016.

Guller, M. & Guller, M. (2003) From Airport to airport city. Editional Gustavo , Gili, Barcel on a.Intervistas Consulting Inc.

Massachusetts Institute Of Technology (MIT), Lean Aerospace Initiative, Available: www.lean.mit.edu, 2005.

CHAPTER FOUR

Airport organizational long term strategy plan

What does airport long term strategy plan? The analysis of the Airport services has been based around what Inxure refers to as the 'Value Model'. The model is represented in the following diagram. The purpose of the model is to enable a structured and coherent consideration of the important facets which must align and culminate toallow the airport services to provide value to CHRC and the central highlands region. The strategy to any country airport may include as below:

•Assess the current state of the
business and its service
outcomes

•Set goals & objectives the
Airport

•Base this on Council plans and
input from various Council
stakeholders
Future

•Develop a work program to
bridge the gap between current
state and future aspirations for
the Airport

•Prioritise the program based on
risk

Airport Operational Trends

Unlike major capital city airports that typically experience some level of linear growth in passenger movements over successive years, regional airports such as Emerald are subject to a range of influences that lead to

greater fluctuations in usage over time. Passenger numbers at Emerald are influenced by changes in local population, regional workforce development, tourism development,
local events, resource trends and construction cycles and the availability of government services
such as health and access to professional services. A further factor that will impact on future revenue
passenger numbers includes the ongoing provision of scheduled airlines services with appropriate
levels of service including price and frequency to attract prospective users.
SWOT Analysis
A high level, strategic level assessment of the strengths, weaknesses, opportunities and threats for
the Airport has been developed as follows. This SWOT analysis has been considered in the
development of the Business and Operating Models for the business plan.
The Value Model sees the purpose (or vision and strategy) being made up of:
• A clear overall strategic direction or vision for the Airport;
• An understanding of how it links to Council's overall Strategic Framework and then into
tangible and implementable actions and targets; and
• A clear risk appetite and tolerance (i.e. what strategic risks will the organisation take and not
take in respect of the Airport).Components
• Overall Strategic Direction
• Strategy and tactics
• Brand
• Risk Appetite
• Product offerings
• Market strategies and tactics
• Pricing plans
• Customer value propositions
• Financial management
• Resourcing talent management
• Business Systems (Project/Risk/Quality Management)
• Systems

• Governance (Board, Committees, Programs)
• Performance (Value) Measurement
Core Operations & Projects
(Delivery)
Vision &
Strategy
(Purpose)
Business Model
(How value is created)
Operating Model
(How value is delivered)
he key Principles upon which this Plan is based are;
· Implement a safe, secure and environmentally suitable airport;
· Construct a well-planned airport;
· Develop sound asset management and business practices;
· Ensure strong financial viability and sustainability factors; and,
· Focus on branding and marketing.
There are a number of key objectives that can be immediately implemented, and which
are detailed along with specified actions that will result in the development of a dynamic,
financially viable asset for the community.
Future development and growth should be investigated as funding opportunities arise,
and a review of this plan is recommended every five years to determine whether market
forces have changed or business opportunities have arisen that could benefit this Airport facility.
The Strategic Plan articulated three objectives for Cessnock Airport:
· Be a safe and complying facility that minimises negative impacts on residential
amenity;
· Promote economic and tourism development across the local government area;
and
· Provide a sustainable revenue stream.

   Route development programs have become popular with airports worldwide to enhance air connectivity. Enhanced air connectivity of an airport has been found to have a positive and significant impact on the competitiveness and attractiveness of the airport and the regional economy in which the airport is located. However, the drivers behind route development programs and their performance are not always clear; this has been less explored in the literature. A dynamic performance management approach is taken to build a modeling framework in which key drivers affecting route development performance and strategic resources affecting key drivers are identified. Route-level planning is used in an empirical study to demonstrate the dynamic mechanism of airport route development initiatives and performance measurements. The proposed framework can not only provide performance monitoring, but also suggest suitable indicators to evaluate the performance for policymakers in future airport route development.

Airport network connectivity has been viewed as an important factor driving airports' attractiveness to travelers and competitiveness in the industry Theoretically, an accessible and interconnected network will enhance airports' attractiveness; the more attractive the airport, the better its competitive position relative to other surrounding airports serving the same region. The competitive position helps an airport to earn market share and improves productivity through higher passenger volume and freight volume. The increased traffic can leverage commercial revenue for larger airports, but has a lower contribution to regional airports. However, well-connected airports can enhance the national air network efficiency and the development of communities and businesses. Hence, enhancing air connectivity via RD programs has been considered a common strategy for modern airports.

The accumulation and depletion of strategic resources will be affected by the endogenous impacts of the end results. The value of resources in a given time is determined by the strategic policy developed by decision-makers. Then, the resources can be deployed to enhance performance drivers and the intermediate results. Ultimately, this affects the end results. Consequently, organizations will achieve sustainable development via the positive interaction cycles among resources, performance drivers, and end results

In such an environment, aeronautical customers (airlines) and non-aeronautical consumers (passengers) both contribute to enhance and co-create service and product values for airports. Thus, airports have been considered and validated as a two-sided platform instead of a vertical structure . Apart from obtaining revenue from airlines and passengers, the role of airports is to facilitate airlines to provide passengers with air services, and foster a profitable interaction among them, leading to passengers' satisfaction. Particularly, under RD initiatives, airlines are also the partners who contribute to enrich airport services, which attracts more airlines and reinforces airport competition and network effects. In this value chain, passengers are no longer the "passive" consumers located at the end of the value chain because their experience also adds value to airports' service and products. Therefore, on the basis of the <<resources–drivers–outcomes>> logic corresponding to the <<value creation–value capture–outcomes>> process, the value creation, capture, and transfer mechanism of airport RD

Driving factors influencing airport attractiveness are identified and used to track resources and stakeholders. While airport attractiveness is generally conceptualized as driven by straightforward and unambiguous criteria, from the perspective of passenger choices, it could be influenced by the location of an airport, and other utilities passengers gain from services of a particular airport . Location and related factors such as ground transport services are often beyond the control of airports. Hence, airports tend to focus on strategies that can enhance other airport utilities, such as fare level, connectivity, and on-time performance by resident airlines

Meanwhile, flights served by airlines improve airport attractiveness and airport financial performance by increased passenger volume and the subsequent increase in airport revenues. The more connected an airport's network is, the more attractive it is relative to other competing airports in the same region. In addition, the improved network may enhance service level by the airport and stimulate economic growth of the region with more air traffic flow. Thus, routes could be considered a crucial resource and revenue generator for airports. Hence, the conceptual model in Fig 3 can explain why RD is the focus of interest to airport managers and authorities, and provide insights for building the DPM model focusing on the airport RD program.

However, airport attractiveness is determined mainly by three factors, and they are not independent. Within the airport system, air connectivity has various definitions and calculation methods . In general, air connectivity is determined by the number of connections and number of flights, which are directly provided by airlines at an airport to passengers. Airport-fare level is mostly the decision of airlines, which determine the ticket price with consideration to operating costs and market competition. Airport fees account for a large proportion of airline operating costs and affect airfare levels. In terms of on-time performance, airport operating efficiency has effects on on-time performance. In particular, airport capacity utilization affects flight on-time performance and is determined by how the capacity is used by scheduled and operating fight volumes. Therefore, RD influences these three factors directly, which consequently affect airport attractiveness. So, any airport long term strategy plan may include above all elements in order to achieve the airport whole organization operational success.